House of PRAYER

House of PRAYER

The Compelling Argument for Unified Prayer

"Lord, teach us to pray"

Karen M Isenhower

LOST VALLEY BOOKS

This title is also available as a Lost Valley Books ebook.

ISBN: 979-8-9911065-0-4

Requests for information: LostValleyBooks@gmail.com

Copy Editor: David Beauchamp
Cover Design: Sam Isenhower
Author Photograph: Sam Isenhower
Illustrations: Karen M. Isenhower

To my ten grandchildren, my delightful gifts from God
May you continually find yourselves enriched
by growing up in the House of Prayer

CONTENTS

Priority of Prayer

Power of Prayer

Preface

AT AGE SIXTEEN I ENCOUNTERED Jesus Christ in a way that changed my life. The first thing I became interested in as a new believer was prayer. I secretly asked the Lord for a guitar to help me worship Him in song. He surprised me by answering that prayer through my parents to whom I had not spoken my request. That answered prayer sparked my lifelong journey of asking the Lord to teach me how to pray.

Throughout our college years, my husband Steve and I enjoyed rich fellowship with vibrant believers of all backgrounds, where we continually addressed God together in dorms, apartments, and in spontaneous meetups on the University of Kansas campus. These experiences helped frame concepts for me that make prayer with others an essential unifying action for believers.

I am grateful to my friends at *Moms In Prayer International* for giving me a strong framework for unified prayer. I had the honor of serving in the ministry of MIPI as an Area Coordinator, State Coordinator, Regional Director, and National Director over a period of years. Helping women learn to pray for their children and schools gave me invaluable experience in communicating the most important things about praying with other believers. Much of what I learned in those years is integrated in my thinking about unified prayer.

As I regularly read the whole Bible, I find insights relevant to prayer. I have collected many of these thoughts and arranged them in this book as a compelling argument for unified prayer. Using Scripture as a blueprint for building the House of Prayer, I show you how to lay a foundation, set up a framework, and put building blocks in place. Jesus Christ is the Cornerstone on which this House of Prayer is established. I wrote this book to be a guide to ignite a culture of prayer in any community of believers.

May the Lord reveal Himself to you as the Teacher of Prayer, and may He ignite a prayer revival in your community through people like you.

Prayerfully Yours, Karen

HOUSE OF PRAYER

How to Get the Most from this Book

AS AN INDIVIDUAL

FIRST, READ THE BOOK. Take time to reflect on the questions at the end of each chapter. You can skip over the Group Guide for Unified Prayer.

Secondly, pray as you read the book. Ask the Lord to teach you what He wants you to understand.

Thirdly, share what you learn with someone else, like your pastor, ministry leader, small group leader, Sunday School teacher, or ordinary brother or sister in Christ. To make it easy, just share the book with them.

Lastly, answer the questions for the *Practical Challenge* at the end of the book, and plant your THREE SEEDS in the ground through prayer.

AS A GROUP

EACH OF THE SEVEN CHAPTERS is followed by a *Group Review and Unified Prayer Guide* which includes:

- ***Chapter Review***
- ***Let's Talk About It*** and ***Let's Talk About It More***
- ***Unified Prayer Guide***

Plan 45 minutes to an hour to complete the three elements of the *Group Review and Unified Prayer Guide.*

You can go through the *Group Review and Unified Prayer Guide* with or without a designated group leader.

- If you have a designated group leader, that person can lead the group or ask someone else to lead the group through the *Group Review and Unified Prayer Guide.*

• If you do not have a designated group leader, you can share the responsibilities of reading the *Chapter Review*, asking the questions in *Let's Talk About It*, talking through the *Prayer Guide*, and initiating and closing the prayer times in Unified Prayer.

Choose one of these four study plans:

Seven-week study

Every person reads one chapter each week and comes ready to review the chapter and talk about it in the group, and then participates in Unified Prayer.

Seven-week study, simplified

The leader of the group reads the chapter and then leads the group through the *Group Review and Unified Prayer Guide*. Encourage each person in the group to read all seven chapters on their own.

Three-week study (Chapters 4, 5, 6)

The leader of the group reads all seven chapters. Every person reads one chapter (4, 5, 6) each week and comes ready to review the chapter and talk about it in the group, and then participates in Unified Prayer. Encourage each person in the group to read all seven chapters on their own.

Three-week study, simplified (Chapters 4, 5, 6)

The leader of the group reads all seven chapters, and then leads the group through the *Group Review and Unified Prayer Guide* for chapters 4, 5, and 6. Encourage each person in the group to read all seven chapters on their own.

May your yearning for God's will to be done never wane.

Purpose of Prayer

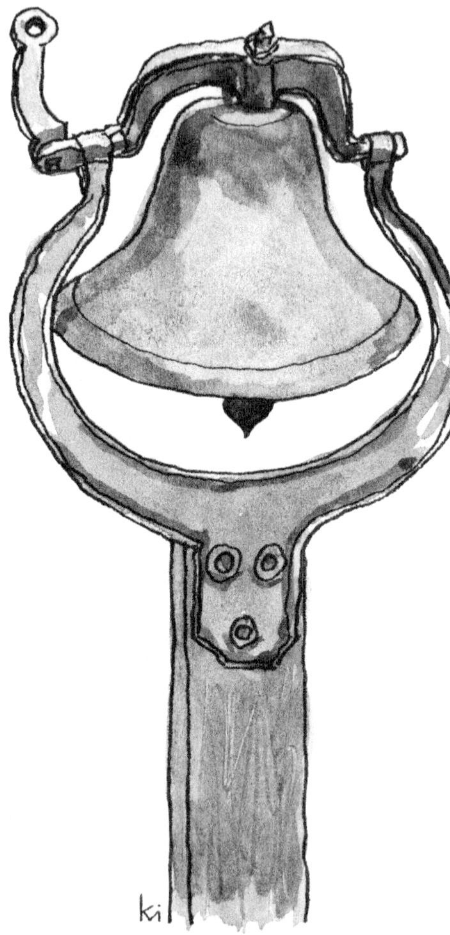
ki

1. Call to Prayer

Shower, O heavens, from above, and let the clouds rain down righteousness; let the earth open, that salvation and righteousness may bear fruit; let the earth cause them both to sprout; I the LORD have created it. (Isaiah 45:8 ESV)

WHY PRAY?

Accomplish God's Will

GOD ACCOMPLISHES HIS WILL through prayers of His people. When we pray according to His will He hears us and responds to our prayers. His answers are always in line with His purposes. God looks for those who are interested in seeing His will be done here on earth. For this reason, we must make the understanding of His will our main pursuit.

> Pray like this: Our Father in heaven, your name be honored as holy. Your kingdom come. Your will be done on earth as it is in heaven. (Matthew 6:9 - 10)

We know His will regarding those who are away from Him. He wants lost souls to receive His salvation through repentance. "The Lord does not delay his promise, as some understand delay, but is patient with you, not wanting any to perish but all to come to repentance." (2 Peter 3:9) "This is good, and it pleases God our Savior, who wants everyone to be saved and to come to the knowledge of the truth." (1 Timothy 2:3 - 4)

God is looking for believers who pray. We have the high privilege of bringing critical needs to God. He is inviting us to petition Him to restore, heal, rescue, bring light into the darkness, break bondages of sin, and move mountains! Where are the gaps in the wall? Where has the enemy torn walls down? Where is sin overtaking a generation of young people? Go find the gaps in order to restore the wall. "You did not go up to the gaps or restore the wall around the house of Israel so that it might stand in battle on the day of the Lord." (Ezekiel 13:5)

Is there anyone who will find the gaps in the wall and stand in the gap to plead for God's mercy? Sin has broken down the protective wall and there is nothing to keep God's justice from bringing judgment. God looked for someone among the people of Israel to intercede for the sinful city but found not one. "I searched for a man among them who would repair the wall and stand in the gap before me on behalf of the land so that I might not destroy it, but I found no one." (Ezekiel 22:30)

You can be that one. So can I. But how? We need help to know how to pray for the most pressing needs. "In the same way the Spirit also helps us in our weakness, because we do not know what to pray for as we should, but the Spirit himself intercedes for us with inexpressible groanings. And he who searches our hearts knows the mind of the Spirit, because he intercedes for the saints according to the will of God." (Romans 8:26 - 27)

We want to know how to pray in a direct line to God, full of faith. The Holy Spirit intercedes for us so we can know God's will. This empowers our faith for praying with confidence to know that God hears.

> Who is the one who condemns? Christ Jesus is the one who died, but even more, has been raised; he also is at the right hand of God and intercedes for us. Who can separate us from the love of Christ? Can affliction or distress or persecution or famine or nakedness or danger or sword? As it is written: Because of you we are being put to death all day long; we are counted as sheep to be slaughtered. No, in all these things we are more than conquerors through him who loved us. (Romans 8:34 - 37)

We want to know how to pray with right motives. Jesus intercedes for us so that we can remain strong in God's love. This stirs a heart of compassion in us for praying in line with God's will for people and for every circumstance we encounter. The Holy Spirit is interceding for you. Jesus is interceding for you. Prayer is the means for God's will to be accomplished in your life. "So he [Jesus] is able to save completely those who come to God through him, because he always lives to intercede for them. For it is indeed fitting for us to have such a high priest: holy, innocent, undefiled, separate from sinners, and exalted above the heavens." (Hebrews 7:25 - 26 NET)

With Christ in us, we, too, have the desire to see God's will accomplished in the lives of people we know. Paul gives Epaphras as an example of someone who wants to see God's will in the lives of those for whom he is praying. "Epaphras, who is one of you, a servant of Christ Jesus, sends you greetings. He is always wrestling for you in his prayers, so that you can stand mature and fully assured in everything God wills." (Colossians 4:12)

Our prayers of faith are spiritual avenues for God to reach into and through human experiences. Our wrestling in prayer gets God's full attention.

"Therefore, brothers and sisters, in view of the mercies of God, I urge you to present your bodies as a living sacrifice, holy and pleasing to God; this is your true worship. Do not be conformed to this age, but be transformed by the renewing of your mind, so that you may discern what is the good, pleasing, and perfect will of God." (Romans 12:1 - 2) Renew your mind. ("Let God transform you into a new person by changing the way you think." NLT) Find out the will of God so you can pray appropriately.

"For by the grace given to me, I tell everyone among you not to think of himself more highly than he should think. Instead, think sensibly, as God has distributed a measure of faith to each one." (Romans 12:3) You are less important than you think. You are busy doing things that you think you must do. In reality, someone else could take your place and do most of those things.

You are more important than you think. You underestimate your value in being the one to stand in the gap with faith. You may be the one to awaken another believer to faithfulness in prayer. You may be the one to pray for God's will to be done where no one else has prayed. You may be the one to pray for someone who has never had someone pray for them.

> For you are saved by grace through faith, and this is not from yourselves; it is God's gift—not from works, so that no one can boast. For we are his workmanship, created in Christ Jesus for good works, which God prepared ahead of time for us to do. (Ephesians 2:8 - 10)

The Lord has work for you—specifically you—as a functioning member of His body. "Now as we have many parts in one body, and all the parts do not have the same function, in the same way we who are many are one body in Christ and individually members of one another." (Romans 12:4 - 5)

Of all the things we could be doing, the one thing that has no substitute, no shortcut, and no detour is developing a personal relationship with the Lord through time with Him in prayer. "Rejoice in hope; be patient in affliction; be persistent in prayer." (Romans 12:12) "This is the confidence we have before him: If we ask anything according to his will, he hears us. And if we know that he hears whatever we ask, we know that we have what we have asked of him." (1 John 5:14 - 15)

Meet with Jesus

What are your prayer habits? Some people answer by saying they talk to Jesus all day long, that they are constantly praying about everything they are doing. What does it say if we "take Jesus with us wherever we go," but neglect to come and sit still with Jesus long enough to have a meaningful conversation? We offer our Lord Jesus Christ the first fruits of our day as a way to yield to His plans. Instead of "taking Jesus with us" we want to be following His steps.

> Come to me, all of you who are weary and burdened, and I will give you rest. Take my yoke upon you and learn from me, because I am lowly and humble in heart, and you will find rest for your souls. For my yoke is easy and my burden is light. (Matthew 11:28 - 30)

"Come to me, all of you who are weary and burdened, and I will give you rest." We meet with Jesus when weary and burdened, and receive rest as

we sit at His feet. "The next day John saw Jesus coming toward him and said, 'Look, the Lamb of God, who takes away the sin of the world!'" (John 1:29)

IT IS THROUGH PRAYER
THAT WE ANSWER HIS CALL
TO COME TO HIM

"Take my yoke upon you." A yoke sits on the shoulders of a load-carrying animal, or on a pair of beasts of burden. Jesus takes our load of sin off us and gives us His yoke to put on instead. We have rest for our souls because it is not our human efforts that make us right with God, it is His grace. His yoke of grace connects us with Him as we pray.

"Learn from me, because I am lowly and humble in heart." Walk in close coordination with Jesus' steps to be discipled by Him. A disciple wants to learn and is taught by the Lord through intimate times in prayer.

"For my yoke is easy and my burden is light." He has work for us to do, but we carry out assignments in Jesus' name. We pray as He leads us to pray. Jesus frees us from the heavy burden of sin as we repent and lifts the load of worry as we bring our concerns to Him in prayer.

Jesus is lowly and humble in heart. This is the yoke He wants us to put on. His yoke is easy, and it lightens the load. Humility is our restraint and our freedom.

"Or do you despise the riches of his kindness, restraint, and patience, not recognizing that God's kindness is intended to lead you to repentance?" (Romans 2:4) God's kind patience with us leads us to repentance from sin. His yoke that we put on is a continuation of His kind patience with us that guides us to conform to His ways. We walk with Jesus to be representatives of God's kindness that leads people to repentance. We pray for God's kindness to reach more people in life-transforming ways.

> As a deer longs for flowing streams, so I long for you, God. I thirst for God, the living God. When can I come and appear before God? (Psalm 42:1 - 2)

> I will bless the Lord who counsels me—even at night when my thoughts trouble me. I always let the Lord guide me. Because he is at my right hand, I will not be shaken. Therefore my heart is glad and my whole being rejoices; my body also rests securely. For you will not abandon me to Sheol; you will not allow your faithful one to see decay. You reveal the path of life to me; in your presence is abundant joy; at your right hand are eternal pleasures. (Psalm 16:7 - 11)

Live by Faith

In prayer we express confidence in the Lord by saying out loud what is true about the Lord. This is more than thinking good things about God. This is specifically putting words to what we know in our heart.

> So don't throw away your confidence, which has a great reward. For you need endurance, so that after you have done God's will, you may receive what was promised. For yet in a very little while, the Coming One will come and not delay. But my righteous one will live by faith; and if he draws back, I have no pleasure in him. But we are not those who draw back and are destroyed, but those who have faith and are saved. (Hebrews 10:35 - 39)

Does a true believer in Jesus want to go through life with minimal conversational time with the Lord? Who wants to miss the glorious abundant grace available for daily victory in Christ? A prayerless life is an unexamined life. It is in prayer that we come near to the Lord for the examination of the desires and thoughts of our heart.

> May the words of my mouth and the meditation of my heart be acceptable to you, LORD, my rock and my Redeemer. (Psalm 19:14)

Living without this essential relationship-development time with the Lord is a self-reliant way to live. If this describes you, come on into the intimacy with God for which you are designed. Humble yourself to admit neglecting this priority. Be washed in God's mercy again.

"He [Jesus] said to him, 'Love the Lord your God with all your heart, with all your soul, and with all your mind.'" (Matthew 22:37) Ask the Lord to awaken you to His presence, so that you will love Him with all your heart, soul, and mind. The Holy Spirit keeps beckoning us to come closer to the Lord. He invites us to live by faith in Christ. This is your most important prayer right now. Please pause to pray. Ask the Lord to 'direct your heart to God's love and Christ's endurance' (from 2 Thessalonians 3:5).

> No creature is hidden from him, but all things are naked and exposed to the eyes of him to whom we must give an account. Therefore, since we have a great high priest who has passed through the heavens—Jesus the Son of God—let us hold fast to our confession. For we do not have a high priest who is unable to sympathize with our weaknesses, but one who has been tempted in every way as we are, yet without sin. Therefore, let us approach the throne of grace with boldness, so that we may receive mercy and find grace to help us in time of need. (Hebrews 4:13 - 16)

God, Creator of the universe and King of kings, welcomes us to approach His holy throne. How do we do that? We do not physically walk up to God's throne, do we? Then, by what means do we go to His throne? Prayer is the red carpet that leads directly to the throne of grace, where we confidently approach our King with faith to receive the help we need.

SATURATE THE SOUL

Intentionally Unhurried

I LEARNED FROM MY GREEN-THUMB MOTHER to water plants slowly and to thoroughly saturate the soil. A little water at the surface now and then may well keep the plant alive. For the plant to flourish, however, the soil must be saturated deep down to the roots.

> "For my thoughts are not your thoughts, and your ways are not my ways." This is the Lord's declaration. "For as heaven is higher than earth, so my ways are higher than your ways, and my thoughts than your thoughts. For just as rain and snow fall from heaven and do not return there without saturating the earth and making it germinate and sprout, and providing seed to sow and food to eat, so my word that comes from my mouth will not return to me empty, but it will accomplish what I please and will prosper in what I send it to do." (Isaiah 55:8 - 11)

Are we satisfied with prayers that merely dampen the soil on the surface? How much more satisfying it is when our prayers deeply saturate the soil! A little prayer does a little good, like sprinkling the top of the soil when we walk by the drooping plant. In contrast, prayer that is intentionally unhurried brings God's peace that goes deep into a person's roots and waters the soul. This is the prayer of which we desperately need to be a part. Prayer that aligns our desires with God's desires is prayer that enters the presence of God. This slow-watering kind of prayer is prayer in which the Lord's presence saturates a thirsty soul. Linger in prayer. Allow time for the Lord to reveal His presence to you.

SATURATE EVERY NEED IN PRAYER
BY BEING INTENTIONALLY UNHURRIED

We need people who pray. It is more than talking about prayer, believing in prayer, or even explaining about prayer. Are we the people who take time to pray? Everything else on our to-do lists is important. In *Quiet Talks on Prayer*, S. D. Gordon writes, "We haven't time. Life is so crowded. This something else is important. Very important, and pressing, but still less important and less pressing than prayer."[1]

"Whoever brings blessing will be enriched, and one who waters will himself be watered." (Proverbs 11:25 ESV) Pray for others as if you are bringing them water in a desert. Our prayers are an important part of serving others. As we pay attention to needs of people around us—struggling marriages, long-term health concerns, major decisions, and the daily ups and downs of life, we see much to bring to the Lord on their behalf. It is not unusual in these times of prayer that we come to understand our part in serving them with physical help, as well.

Saturation of the soil produces fruit that grows with a bounty of seeds to sow. Saturation of the soul produces fruit with seeds to sow into souls for God's kingdom.

God's Word Lights the Way

Include God's word in your prayers, knowing that His word is true. God's words fall like rain to saturate the soul and bring spiritual growth in people's lives. His word guides us to walk in His ways and to stay on His path. This is the perfect place from which to start our prayers. "Your word is a lamp for my feet and a light on my path." (Psalm 119:105)

Our Bibles are rich with prayer examples, and with inspired words for earthly circumstances.

For leaders in the church:

"Preach the word; be ready in season and out of season; correct, rebuke, and encourage with great patience and teaching." (2 Timothy 4:2)

"Lord, guide our pastor in his study of Your word for the preaching You have called him to do. Give him the needed skills to know how to correct someone when needed, to know when it's time to offer a rebuke, and give him the words to encourage those You put in his path today."

For parents:

"Fathers, don't stir up anger in your children, but bring them up in the training and instruction of the Lord." (Ephesians 6:4)

"Lord, please teach my friend how to train and instruct his young children in a way that honors You."

For people searching for meaning:

"For it was you who created my inward parts; you knit me together in my mother's womb. I will praise you because I have been remarkably and wondrously made. Your works are wondrous, and I know this very well. My bones were not hidden from you when I was made in secret, when I was formed in the depths of the earth. Your eyes saw me when I was formless; all my days were written in your book and planned before a single one of them began." (Psalm 139:13 - 16)

"Lord, You saw my relative before she was born. Lead her to understand how her life fits in your plan. Please awaken her to search for meaning in You, Jesus Christ."

For persecuted Christians:

"You are being guarded by God's power through faith for a salvation that is ready to be revealed in the last time. You rejoice in this, even though now for a short time, if necessary, you suffer grief in various trials so that the proven character of your faith—more valuable than gold which, though perishable, is refined by fire—may result in praise, glory, and honor at the revelation of Jesus Christ. Though you have not seen him, you love him; though not seeing him now, you believe in him, and you rejoice with inexpressible and glorious joy, because you are receiving the goal of your faith, the salvation of your souls." (1 Peter 1:5 - 9)

"Lord, as we hear of our brothers and sisters in Christ in the nation of _______ suffering for the name of Jesus, we ask that You would guard their hearts by Your power. Strengthen them in their faith, preserving them for the salvation to come."

Praying from these starting points in Scripture is a purposeful way for us to come before the Lord. As we read Scripture, we can be attentive to those passages that open up a conversation for us with the Lord.

Total Trust

When we have total trust in the Lord there are times that we saturate the ground with our tears in prayer. We pour out our hearts before Him, letting our words to the Lord flow from deep within. We tell Him we need Him. When we allow tears to express sincere emotion we give the Lord access to the most vulnerable places in our hearts. This total trust is faith that pleases the Lord. As the Lord comforts us in our troubles, He strengthens us to comfort others in His name.

> Trust in him at all times, you people; pour out your hearts before him. God is our refuge. Selah (Psalm 62:8)

> Blessed be the God and Father of our Lord Jesus Christ, the Father of mercies and the God of all comfort. He comforts us in all our affliction, so that we may be able to comfort those who are in any kind of affliction, through the comfort we ourselves receive from God. (2 Corinthians 1:3 - 4)

When we pour out our hearts for others, we carry the burden for them until they make it through their hardship. God hears our prayers and intervenes in their circumstances. When we understand that our prayers help these individuals put their hope in God, we press in to saturate the ground with our tears even more.

> We don't want you to be unaware, brothers and sisters, of our affliction that took place in Asia. We were completely overwhelmed—beyond our strength—so that we even despaired of life itself. Indeed, we felt that we had received the sentence of death, so that we would not trust in ourselves but in God who raises the dead. He has delivered us from such a terrible death, and he will deliver us. We have put our hope in him that he will deliver us again while you join in helping us by your prayers. Then many will give thanks on our behalf for the gift that came to us through the prayers of many. (2 Corinthians 1:8 - 11)

We do not often know when someone is completely overwhelmed, and in despair, like apostle Paul and his companions were. Paul attributes the prayers of his brothers and sisters in Christ to bringing hope of God's deliverance to them. Our prayers matter! Let our prayers of faith carry those who need hope through their circumstances. Let our afflicted brothers and sisters in Christ trust us to pray with total trust in the Lord on their behalf.

> God, you are my God; I eagerly seek you. I thirst for you; my body faints for you in a land that is dry, desolate, and without water. (Psalm 63:1)

> The one who lives under the protection of the Most High dwells in the shadow of the Almighty. I will say concerning the LORD, who is my refuge

> and my fortress, my God in whom I trust: He himself will rescue you from the bird trap, from the destructive plague. He will cover you with his feathers; you will take refuge under his wings. His faithfulness will be a protective shield. (Psalm 91:1 - 4)

WHY PRAY TOGETHER?

Strength in Unity

PETER, JOHN, JAMES, ANDREW, Philip, Thomas, Bartholomew, Matthew, James, Simon, and Judas son of James were in the upstairs room in Jerusalem. They went to this room after they had watched Jesus disappear from sight, having been lifted up into the clouds. In that room upstairs they prayed together. They were joined by some women, including Mary the mother of Jesus. Jesus' brothers were there, too. "These all with one mind were continually devoting themselves to prayer" (Acts 1:14 NASB).

What was it like to be in that room? Can you imagine the vibrancy of expectation in the air? What is it like to participate with a roomful of people who are all in agreement waiting to see the power of God, waiting for the promised indwelling of the Holy Spirit, waiting for the unknown? What does it look like and sound like for believers in Jesus to persist in unhurried prayer together with one mind? This scenario is a shocking contrast to the days when the disciples were terrified and locked in hiding prior to Jesus' appearance to them. Now that all these people truly believe in Jesus' words about the Father's promise, they are energized with high anticipation. And they are praying.

Does it mean there is a roomful of people all praying silent prayers at the same time? Does it mean there is a roomful of people all praying separate prayers aloud at the same time? Does it mean one leader is praying and everyone else is nodding in agreement?

What if it means that everyone contributes to the prayer together, as family, united?

Could it be that the Holy Spirit forms the prayer in the hearts and minds of those believers in the room, according to the Father's will, and gives thoughts to turn into words? One speaks, and then another, and then another? Imagine each spoken prayer harmonizing with the ones already expressed, until the fullness of the body of Christ is seen in all her unified beauty. This is a House of Prayer that is rich with kingdom objectives. This is where requests are deeply saturated in prayer as believers come together before the throne of God.

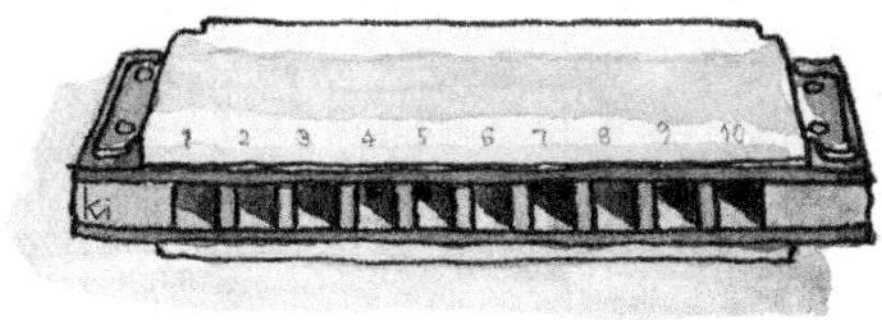

EACH SPOKEN PRAYER HARMONIZES WITH THE ONES ALREADY EXPRESSED

Stand With One Another

We speak honestly with each other to invite prayer, knowing that the Lord brings healing where we need it through the prayers of our brothers and sisters in Christ. We pray with and for one another, knowing our prayers are effective for bringing God's will into any situation.

> Therefore, confess your sins to one another and pray for one another, so that you may be healed. The prayer of a righteous person is very powerful in its effect. (James 5:16)

> Rejoice always, pray constantly, give thanks in everything; for this is God's will for you in Christ Jesus. (1 Thessalonians 5:16 - 18)

We pray together because our faith is strengthened through hearts that are united in Christ for a purpose. This is how we handle celebration and adversity in the body of Christ. We pray together to give thanks, and we pray together to ask God to intervene.

When Peter is arrested after the execution of fellow-believer James, Peter's believing friends recognize it as a crisis. They gather together to pray for Peter. God hears their prayer and intervenes in a miraculous way.

Peter is led out of prison by an angel and goes to where the believers are in prayer. "When Peter realized this, he went to the house of Mary, the mother of John Mark, where many people had gathered together and were praying." (Acts 12:12 NET)

The prayer of gathered believers interrupts the adversary's scheme to silence the gospel. Our prayers matter.

Nehemiah organized crews all along the broken walls and gates in Jerusalem for a huge restoration project. Opposition was fierce, with derision, threats, and darts of discouragement that were constantly aimed at the building crews. Nehemiah found a way to keep everyone strong for rebuilding the wall despite the enemy's schemes. Nehemiah had the builders carry weapons and he had someone blow a ram's horn to call everyone together at key times.

> Each of the builders had his sword strapped around his waist while he was building, and the one who sounded the ram's horn was beside me. Then I said to the nobles, the officials, and the rest of the people, "The work is enormous and spread out, and we are separated far from one another along the wall. Wherever you hear the sound of the ram's horn, rally to us there. Our God will fight for us!" (Nehemiah 4:18 - 20)

We need each other. The work we have been given to do is enormous and we are spread out. We are each separately doing the work we are assigned to do. Our weapon is the word of God, and our call is to rally together in prayer. Listen for the call to prayer. We must come together to pray. Here, in the House of Prayer, we are strengthened and encouraged for the work we are doing. We are reminded that we are united, with God fighting our battles for us.

> Pray at all times in the Spirit with every prayer and request, and stay alert with all perseverance and intercession for all the saints. Pray also for me, that the message may be given to me when I open my mouth to make known with boldness the mystery of the gospel. (Ephesians 6:18 - 19)

HOUSE OF PRAYER

THREE CONCEPTS FROM SCRIPTURE become building blocks for effective prayer of gathered believers: Together, Family, Unity. "So, then, you are no longer foreigners and strangers, but fellow citizens with the saints, and members of God's household, built on the foundation of the apostles and prophets, with Christ Jesus himself as the cornerstone." (Ephesians 2:19 - 20)

Together

We are together in the body of Christ.

> And he himself gave some to be apostles, some prophets, some evangelists, some pastors and teachers, to equip the saints for the work of ministry, to build up the body of Christ, until we all reach unity in the faith and in the knowledge of God's Son, growing into maturity with a stature measured by Christ's fullness. Then we will no longer be little children, tossed by the waves and blown around by every wind of teaching, by human cunning with cleverness in the techniques of deceit. But speaking the truth in love, let us grow in every way into him who is the head—Christ. From him the whole body, fitted and knit together by every supporting ligament, promotes the growth of the body for building itself up in love by the proper working of each individual part. (Ephesians 4:11 - 16)

Linger in Unified Prayer to saturate dry ground around you. Enjoy taking your time in prayer, hearing each other's voices. As people in the room take turns to contribute their words in prayer, we get to experience the beauty of the Bride of Christ in the presence of the Lord.

Family

Unified Prayer is like a family conversation. "Don't rebuke an older man, but exhort him as a father, younger men as brothers, older women as mothers, and the younger women as sisters with all purity." (1 Timothy 5:1 - 2) We get a taste of the flavor of relationships that Paul developed while he was in Rome. This is what family is like.

Paul describes this family of believers: "sister... who is a servant of the church... coworkers in Christ Jesus, who risked their own necks for my life... the church that meets in their home... my dear friend who is the first convert to Christ from Asia... one who has worked very hard for you... my fellow Jews and fellow prisoners... my dear friend in the Lord... our coworker in Christ... my dear friend... one who is approved in Christ... those who belong to a certain household... my fellow Jew... those in a certain household who are in the Lord... those who have worked hard in the Lord... my dear friend who has worked hard in the Lord... chosen in the Lord... a mother to me... brothers and sisters... and all the saints who are with them." (Romans 16:1 - 23, excerpts)

Unity

We come together in unity. "Above all, put on love, which is the perfect bond of unity. And let the peace of Christ, to which you were also called in one body, rule your hearts. And be thankful." (Colossians 3:14 - 15)

> *You visit the earth and water it abundantly, enriching it greatly. God's stream is filled with water, for you prepare the earth in this way, providing people with grain. You soften it with showers and bless its growth, soaking its furrows and leveling its ridges. You crown the year with your goodness; your carts overflow with plenty. The wilderness pastures overflow, and the hills are robed with joy. The pastures are clothed with flocks and the valleys covered with grain. They shout in triumph; indeed, they sing. (Psalm 65:9 - 13)*

Group Review and Unified Prayer Guide

Chapter 1: Call to Prayer

INSTRUCTIONS:

- Read through the chapter review together.
- Please reserve ample time at the end of your gathering for unhurried Unified Prayer (15-30 minutes suggested).

Chapter Review

Why pray?

We have good reasons to pray. We pray because we are interested that God's will be done. God accomplishes his will through prayers of His people, so we want to be available as His praying servants.

We also pray to meet with Jesus. It is through prayer that we answer His call to come to Him, learn from Him, and walk with Him.

Prayer is an expression of our faith. We show our dependence on the Lord when we acknowledge our need in prayer and accept His will for every facet of our lives.

Saturate the soul.

Just as slow watering saturates a thirsty plant, we can saturate every need in prayer by being intentionally unhurried.

We allow God's word to saturate our lives so we can pray according to His will. Besides being rich with prayer examples, our Bibles give us wording and thoughts for inspired praying.

Our prayers clear a path for others to gain hope in life's afflictions. We carry faith for those who are weak, knowing that God intervenes at the right time.

Why pray together?

There is strength in unity. The body of Christ experiences unity when we come together in prayer before the throne of God.

We pray with and for one another to ask the Lord to accomplish his will in every situation. Our faith is strengthened as we stand with one another in Christ.

Let's Talk About It

INSTRUCTIONS:

- Read each Scripture.
- Use the accompanying question to discuss how the Scripture relates to prayer.

"Come to me, all of you who are weary and burdened, and I will give you rest. Take my yoke upon you and learn from me, because I am lowly and humble in heart, and you will find rest for your souls. For my yoke is easy and my burden is light." (Matthew 11:28 - 30)

What does Jesus ask us to do? What exchange does He want to make with us?

"Your word is a lamp for my feet and a light on my path." (Psalm 119:105)

In what way is God's word a good starting place for our prayers?

"These all with one mind were continually devoting themselves to prayer" (Acts 1:14 NASB).

What do these believers gain by being all with one mind? How is the fullness of the body of Christ displayed when we pray together, as family, united?

Let's Talk About It More (as time allows)

"Pray like this: Our Father in heaven, your name be honored as holy. Your kingdom come. Your will be done on earth as it is in heaven." (Matthew 6:9 - 10)

Why is our understanding of our Heavenly Father's will important for prayer?

"No creature is hidden from him, but all things are naked and exposed to the eyes of him to whom we must give an account. Therefore, since we have a great high priest who has passed through the heavens—Jesus the Son of God—let us hold fast to our confession. For we do not have a high priest who is unable to sympathize with our weaknesses, but one who has been tempted in every way as we are, yet without sin. Therefore, let us approach the throne of grace with boldness, so that we may receive mercy and find grace to help us in time of need." (Hebrews 4:13 - 16)

We do not physically walk up to God's throne, do we? By what means, then, do we approach the throne of grace? What do we receive when we come to His throne?

"'For my thoughts are not your thoughts, and your ways are not my ways.' This is the Lord's declaration. 'For as heaven is higher than earth, so my ways are higher than your ways, and my thoughts than your thoughts. For just as rain and snow fall from heaven and do not return there without saturating the earth and making it germinate and sprout, and providing seed to sow and food to eat, so my word that comes from my mouth will not return to me empty, but it will accomplish what I please and will prosper in what I send it to do.'" (Isaiah 55:8 - 11)

For what purpose do the rain and snow saturate the earth? Compare God's word to rain and snow. What results from unhurried prayers that saturate the needs we bring to the Lord?

"We don't want you to be unaware, brothers and sisters, of our affliction that took place in Asia. We were completely overwhelmed—beyond our strength—so that we even despaired of life itself. Indeed, we felt that we had received the sentence of death, so that we would not trust in ourselves but in God who raises the dead. He has delivered us from such a terrible death, and he will deliver us. We have put our hope in him that he will deliver us again while you join in helping us by your prayers. Then many will give thanks on our behalf for the gift that came to us through the prayers of many." (2 Corinthians 1:8 - 11)

In what ways do our prayers help someone facing affliction?

"Therefore, confess your sins to one another and pray for one another, so that you may be healed. The prayer of a righteous person is very powerful in its effect." (James 5:16)

How does praying *with* each other help us pray *for* each other? What does the effective prayer of a righteous person accomplish?

Unified Prayer Building Blocks

Together:
Pray short simple prayers from the heart. Include all who want to participate.

Family:
This is a prayer conversation. Take turns. Pray one subject at a time. Listen attentively.

Unity:
Support each other with your prayers. Expound on each prayer as the Holy Spirit leads.

Let's Pray Now!

1 Call to Prayer

Unified Prayer Guide:

INSTRUCTIONS:

- Talk through this guide together.
- Pray, implementing what you have learned.

First Step.

Each person writes down hopes and obstacles regarding their personal prayer habits. For example, "I hope to become consistent with daily prayer." "My busy schedule is an obstacle for me to be devoted to prayer." "I hope to be able to pray out loud with others."

____

Have a group conversation regarding desires you each have about learning to pray alone and learning to pray with other believers.

Next Step.

Include the Lord in your conversation. Ask the Lord to lead the group in Unified Prayer through the guidance of His Holy Spirit.

One person speaks up to say a short simple request to the Lord about one of the hopes or obstacles that he or she has written down. Two or three others in the group take turns to agree with the request by repeating the prayer in their own words.

When there is a pause, someone else speaks up to say a short simple request to the Lord, and others in the group speak prayers that agree.

Continue saturating each spoken request with prayer.

Concluding Step.

When you sense that everyone has had their say in the prayer conversation, take a moment to be still in the presence of the Lord.

Someone says a simple concluding sentence to the prayer, such as, "In Jesus' name we pray, Amen."

2. Foundation

WE NEED A FOUNDATION on which to build a whole-hearted practice of prayer among followers of Jesus. We have that foundation through prayer principles we find in God's word. Alone Prayer is essential as a starting point. Unified Prayer is most effective when each of us personally abide with Christ. The House of Prayer is built on these Alone and Unified practices of prayer.

> Another angel, with a golden incense burner, came and stood at the altar. He was given a large amount of incense to offer with the prayers of all the saints on the golden altar in front of the throne. The smoke of the incense, with the prayers of the saints, went up in the presence of God from the angel's hand. (Revelation 8:3 - 4)

WHAT IS ALONE PRAYER?

Alone with God

ALONE PRAYER IS PERSONAL TIME alone with God. A faith-filled believer in Jesus interacts with the Lord by reading His Word, listening for His instruction. We speak words of thanks and praise and verbalize needs and requests that align with God's will. "Both the Spirit and the bride say, 'Come!' Let anyone who hears, say, 'Come!' Let the one who is thirsty come. Let the one who desires take the water of life freely." (Revelation 22:17)

When we are intimate with Him in this way, God changes our desires to align with His will. This alignment of our will forms the basis for our prayers and gives us confidence to pray. "Whenever you pray, you must not be like the hypocrites, because they love to pray standing in the synagogues and on the street corners to be seen by people. Truly I tell you, they have their reward. But when you pray, go into your private room, shut your door, and pray to your Father who is in secret. And your Father who sees in secret will reward you." (Matthew 6:5 - 6)

The reward is fellowship with God. The secret is unhurried time every day, "time enough to forget about how much time it is."[2]

"Yet he [Jesus] often withdrew to deserted places and prayed." (Luke 5:16) Think of the investment of time that Jesus made in Alone Prayer. Why do you think Jesus went to deserted places? Do you think Jesus had so much spare time that it was easy to fit Alone Prayer time in His schedule? We do not have extra time from which to draw for this. In *Quiet Talks on Prayer*, S. D. Gordon says time "must be taken from something else, something important, but still less important than this."[3]

Jesus does not undervalue His relationship with His Father. Jesus purposely aligns His will with the Father's will, even to the point of death. Notice that He does this in prayer. "Father, if you are willing, take this cup away from me—nevertheless, not my will, but yours, be done." (Luke 22:42) "He [Jesus] humbled himself by becoming obedient to the point of death—even to death on a cross." (Philippians 2:8)

We must remain in Jesus. We abide in Him, and He abides in us. This is how we are able to bear fruit in our lives. "Remain in me, and I in you. Just as a branch is unable to produce fruit by itself unless it remains on the vine, neither can you unless you remain in me. I am the vine; you are the branches. The one who remains in me and I in him produces much fruit, because you can do nothing without me." (John 15:4 - 5)

Remaining steadfast in Jesus is how we are able to bear fruit through our prayers. "If you remain in me and my words remain in you, ask whatever you want and it will be done for you. My Father is glorified by this: that you produce much fruit and prove to be my disciples." (John 15:7 - 8)

We remain in close relationship with Jesus by giving up other things to spend time with Him. In this vital relationship with the Lord, we are strengthened by His vast strength. He gives us his indestructible armor for living with His strength through every adversity we face in this world. "Finally, be strengthened by the Lord and by his vast strength. Put on the full armor of God so that you can stand against the schemes of the devil." (Ephesians 6:10 - 11)

Christ gives us His belt, His sandals, His shield, His helmet, and His sword. The Lord equips us with this armor through time with Him in His word where we learn the meaning of truth, righteousness, good news, faith, and salvation. We employ these heavenly pieces of armor as we pray, standing on the firm ground of God's word of truth. We are the Lord's faithful soldiers, waiting for our next assignment at His command.

> Stand, therefore, with truth like a belt around your waist, righteousness like armor on your chest, and your feet sandaled with readiness for the gospel of peace. In every situation take up the shield of faith with which you can extinguish all the flaming arrows of the evil one. Take the helmet of salvation and the sword of the Spirit—which is the word of God. (Ephesians 6:14 - 17)

We take a stand, with His armor on, and now we are fully ready to pray. This is why we must be serious about abiding in Christ. God intends to accomplish His will through the prayers of His strong faithful servants. My son Sam likes to say that "the sword of the Spirit is the word of God, and prayer is the arm that wields the sword."

> Pray at all times in the Spirit with every prayer and request, and stay alert with all perseverance and intercession for all the saints. (Ephesians 6:18)

Undivided Attention

Mary, the sister of Martha, comes as close as she possibly can to Jesus and listens to Him. She listens like a disciple, giving Jesus her focused attention. Undivided attention means purely listening. She is still. Mary is not distracted, pulled away by good works that need to be done. Mary's worker-bee sister tries to interrupt Mary's closeness with Jesus because there are so many preparations that need to be done. Jesus steps in by pointing out to Martha that her attention is on many things, but that her sister Mary is choosing the one thing that is needed.

> Jesus entered a certain village where a woman named Martha welcomed him as a guest. She had a sister named Mary, who sat at the Lord's feet and listened to what he said. But Martha was distracted with all the preparations she had to make, so she came up to him and said, "Lord, don't you care that my sister has left me to do all the work alone? Tell her to help me." But the Lord answered her, "Martha, Martha, you are worried and troubled about many things, but one thing is needed. Mary has chosen the best part; it will not be taken away from her." (Luke 10:38-42 NET)

Martha welcomes Jesus as guest. Mary attends to Jesus as Lord. Alone Prayer is sitting at the feet of Jesus as an attentive disciple. Let us be intentional about sitting at Jesus' feet.

SIT AT JESUS' FEET
TO BE TAUGHT BY HIM

WHAT IS UNIFIED PRAYER?

Address God Together

UNIFIED PRAYER IS THE PRAYER of believers addressing God together. We interact with the Lord and with each other, speaking words of thanks and praise. We join each other to present our needs to God in requests that align with His will. "Devote yourselves to prayer; stay alert in it with thanksgiving. At the same time, pray also for us that God may open a door to us for the word, to speak the mystery of Christ, for which I am in chains, so that I may make it known as I should." (Colossians 4:2 - 4)

We see that Paul asks the Colossian believers to "pray also for us." The people to whom he is writing receive his requests as a good starting point for raising their voices to God together. Leonard Ravenhill is reported to have said, "The true church lives and moves and has its being in prayer."[4]

Many Voices as One Voice

Singing voices and musical instruments joined together can sound like one voice giving praise to God. "The trumpeters and singers joined together to praise and thank the Lord <u>with one voice</u>. They raised their voices, accompanied by trumpets, cymbals, and musical instruments, in praise to the Lord: For he is good; his faithful love endures forever. The temple, the Lord's temple, was filled with a cloud. And because of the cloud, the priests were not able to continue ministering, for the glory of the Lord filled God's temple." (2 Chronicles 5:13 - 14, emphasis added)

Our voices are separate, yet when we pray together we are unified into the sound of one voice. We are one in Christ. This is the miracle of Unified Prayer—many voices become one.

In *With Christ in the School of Prayer*, Andrew Murray asks, "Who can say what power a Church could develop and exercise, if it gave itself to the work of prayer day and night for the coming of the kingdom, for God's power on His servants and His word, for the glorifying of God in the salvation of souls?"[4]

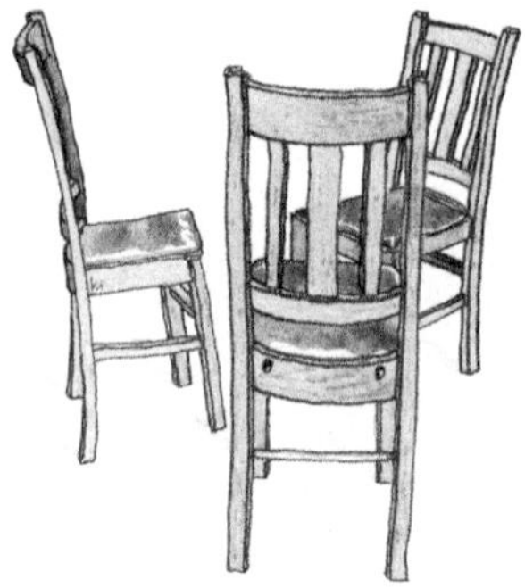

MANY VOICES
COME TOGETHER
AS ONE BEFORE THE LORD

WHAT IS THE HOUSE OF PRAYER?

Practice of Prayer

THE HOUSE OF PRAYER IS ANY PLACE where faith-filled believers in Jesus are gathered together. When we see prayer as the essential unifying action of the body of Christ we are laying the foundation for the House of Prayer. "They all were continually united in prayer, along with the women, including Mary the mother of Jesus, and his brothers." (Acts 1:14)

This is not a call for scheduled prayer meetings. This is a call for prayer wherever believers meet, to make it our common rhythm.

- Make a practice of prayer. Become deliberate about stopping to pray.
- Have a culture of prayer. This is who we are. This is how we operate.
- Prayer is more than a special thing we do together. Prayer is the heartbeat of everything we do together.
- Every gathering is an opportunity for learning to pray together.

Actively look for circumstances that give believers a way to pray together. Make moments of Unified Prayer a part of ordinary occasions. Practice Unified Prayer as a family at home, as a church small group*, or as a volunteer team that is serving in the church or in the community. Practice Unified Prayer in a Sunday School class, staff meeting, worship rehearsal, or team meeting. Practice Unified Prayer in your workplace, at a Bible study, coffee shop, neighborhood gathering, sporting event, children's playground, or during a family celebration. Practice Unified Prayer in any place and for any reason that brings you together with brothers and sisters in Christ.

*Every Christ-centered small group is a greenhouse for prayer-life development.

EVERY CHRIST-CENTERED GROUP
IS A GREENHOUSE FOR PRAYER-LIFE DEVELOPMENT

MY HOUSE WILL BE CALLED A HOUSE OF PRAYER

Honor the Father

JESUS TEACHES US TO HONOR THE FATHER first of all when we pray. Come into the House of Prayer with worship in our hearts and praise on our lips. "So pray this way: Our Father in heaven, may your name be honored." (Matthew 6:9 NET)

We worship God because He is worthy, we praise Him for who He is, and we thank Him for what He is doing, has done, and will do. All attention is on God. We purposely take attention off ourselves. Let us enter our Lord's presence with the honor He deserves as we join the ongoing worship that is continually heard around His throne in heaven.

> Whenever the living creatures give glory, honor, and thanks to the one seated on the throne, the one who lives forever and ever, the twenty-four elders fall down before the one seated on the throne and worship the one who lives forever and ever. They cast their crowns before the throne and say, Our Lord and God, you are worthy to receive glory and honor and power, because you have created all things, and by your will they exist and were created. (Revelation 4:9 - 11)

A pattern we can follow that we see often in Scripture is opening our prayer with words of praise. In this example from Nehemiah, the first words of the prayer express what Nehemiah knows is true about God. Saying what we know is true about God is a pure and simple form of praise, reverently appropriate for coming into God's presence.

"I said, 'Lord, the God of the heavens, the great and awe-inspiring God who keeps his gracious covenant with those who love him and keep his commands'" (Nehemiah 1:5). When we acknowledge God for who He is—how great, strong, and merciful—we begin to see how much we need Him. At this point it is appropriate to bring our needs to Him in prayer, as in the example of Nehemiah's prayer.

"Please, Lord, let your ear be attentive to the prayer of your servant and to that of your servants who delight to revere your name. Give your servant success today, and grant him compassion" (Nehemiah 1:11). This emphasis on praise demonstrates our reliance on the authority of God. We worship the King because we are citizens of His kingdom, and we know He is worthy.

Jesus' love for His Father's house is directly related to His love for the kingdom of God. "Because zeal for your house has consumed me, and the insults of those who insult you have fallen on me." (Psalm 69:9)

Jesus is consumed with zeal for His Father's house. Jesus takes on Himself the insults of those who insult the Father. "'Do you think this temple I have claimed as my own is to be a hideout for robbers? You had better take note! I have seen for myself what you have done!' says the Lord." (Jeremiah 7:11 NET)

Jesus has a desire to honor His Father's house, that it would be a place where all nations may pray. The Father is honored when His people pray together.

> As for the foreigners who join themselves to the Lord to minister to him, to love the name of the Lord, and to become his servants—all who keep the Sabbath without desecrating it and who hold firmly to my covenant—I will bring them to my holy mountain and let them rejoice in my house of prayer. Their burnt offerings and sacrifices will be acceptable on my altar, for my house will be called a house of prayer for all nations. (Isaiah 56:6 - 7)

Prayers as Incense

The prayers of believers are precious to God. Golden bowls at the altar before the Lord hold the prayers of the saints. Incense that rises symbolizes the upward direction of our prayers.

> When he took the scroll, the four living creatures and the twenty-four elders fell down before the Lamb. Each one had a harp and golden bowls filled with incense, which are the prayers of the saints. And they sang a new song: You are worthy to take the scroll and to open its seals, because you were slaughtered, and you purchased people for God by your blood from every tribe and language and people and nation. (Revelation 5:8 - 9)

"Their burnt offerings and sacrifices will be acceptable on my altar, for my house will be called a house of prayer for all nations." (Isaiah 56:7) God made a way for our offerings to be acceptable to Him in His holy house, and for prayers of common people to come to Him without restriction.

"But Jesus cried out again with a loud voice and gave up his spirit. Suddenly, the curtain of the sanctuary was torn in two from top to bottom, the earth quaked, and the rocks were split." (Matthew 27:50 - 51) Jesus opened an unobstructed path to God for us through His blood. The temple curtain was torn as Jesus Christ the Lamb of God was sacrificed for us. The moment of death, when Jesus gave up His spirit, is the moment God opened His kingdom for all who would repent and come to Him through the blood of Jesus. This tearing of the curtain between the holy and the common gave ordinary people access to God. What do we call this access to Almighty God? We call it prayer.

> Therefore, brothers, since we have confidence to enter the holy places by the blood of Jesus, by the new and living way that he opened for us through the curtain, that is, through his flesh, and since we have a great priest over the house of God, let us draw near with a true heart in full assurance of faith, with our hearts sprinkled clean from an evil conscience and our bodies washed with pure water. (Hebrews 10:19 - 22 ESV)

Prayer is the means by which we draw ever nearer to God. When the temple veil was torn as the Lamb of God was sacrificed for us, the prayers from outside the temple became as holy to the Lord as those offered in front of the altar by priests in the temple. Even common cooking pots are now holy when they carry the sacrifices of those coming to God's holy presence. As we draw near to God through the way opened to us by the blood of Jesus, the sacrifice we bring is our repentant heart.

> And on that day there shall be inscribed on the bells of the horses, "Holy to the Lord." And the pots in the house of the Lord shall be as the bowls before the altar. And every pot in Jerusalem and Judah shall be holy to the Lord of hosts, so that all who sacrifice may come and take of them and boil the meat of the sacrifice in them. And there shall no longer be a trader in the house of the Lord of hosts on that day. (Zechariah 14:20 - 21 ESV)

In the Lord's kingdom everything is dedicated to the Lord in holiness for those who have been washed by the blood of the lamb. Now all may come and bring their sacrifices directly to God's altar. And there is no longer a place for traders who come in for other purposes, nor anyone who would interfere with the worship of God in the Father's House of Prayer.

"O Lord, I cry out to you. Come quickly to me. Pay attention to me when I cry out to you. May you accept my prayer like incense, my uplifted hands like the evening offering." (Psalm 141:1 - 2 NET) May the Lord accept our cry for help as a pleasing aroma before His throne. May the Lord see our upraised hands as our willingness to honor Him.

Spiritual Sacrifices

All who humbly present themselves as a living sacrifice are welcome. "Therefore, brothers and sisters, in view of the mercies of God, I urge you to present your bodies as a living sacrifice, holy and pleasing to God; this is your true worship." (Romans 12:1) "The sacrifice God desires is a humble spirit—O God, a humble and repentant heart you will not reject." (Psalm 51:17 NET)

We are the living stones of a spiritual house to be holy priests who offer spiritual sacrifices that please God through Jesus Christ. "As you come to him, a living stone—rejected by people but chosen and honored by God—you yourselves, as living stones, a spiritual house, are being built to be a holy priesthood to offer spiritual sacrifices acceptable to God through Jesus Christ. For it stands in Scripture: See, I lay a stone in Zion, a chosen and honored cornerstone, and the one who believes in him will never be put to shame" (1 Peter 2:4 - 8).

Remove Interference

Let there be no interference in the House of the Prayer. Is there anything that stands in the way for the Lord's children to come directly to Him? If so, eliminate it! "He told those who were selling doves, 'Get these things out of here! Stop turning my Father's house into a marketplace!'" {Jeremiah 7:11; Zechariah 14:21; Malachi 3:1 - 3} "And his disciples remembered that it is written: Zeal for your house will consume me." {Psalm 69:9; Numbers 25:13} (John 2:16 - 17) See also Mark 11:15 - 17; Matthew 21:12 - 13; Luke 19:45 - 46.

"The priests went to the entrance of the Lord's temple to cleanse it. They took all the unclean things they found in the Lord's sanctuary to the courtyard of the Lord's temple. Then the Levites received them and took them outside to the Kidron Valley." (2 Chronicles 29:16) Like these priests during the early part of King Hezekiah's reign in Judah, we, too, must remove everything that does not belong in the Lord's temple. To bring in the ways of the world is to defile God's holy house.

Jesus and His twelve disciples come into Jerusalem and head to the temple. Jesus drives out merchants and consumers. GET OUT! He turns over tables and chairs of religious merchants. NO MORE! He stops all illegitimate traffic from coming through the temple courts. STOP! Then, having everyone's attention, Jesus begins teaching from Scripture: "For my house will be called a house of prayer" (Isaiah 56:7). "Do you think this temple I have claimed as my own is to be a hideout for robbers?" (Jeremiah 7:11)

Firmly determine that nothing will displace prayer in our Father's house. The regular practice of prayer must be primary. Anything less is an insult to the Father. The house is named for what happens in it. This is a House of Prayer. This is where God's grace saturates His children who call on Him.

IS THE HOUSE OF PRAYER A BUILDING?

God's People Together

WE, THE BODY OF CHRIST, are God's temple. Collectively, we are the Father's house. We are the House of Prayer. "Don't you yourselves know that you are God's temple and that the Spirit of God lives in you? If anyone destroys God's temple, God will destroy him; for God's temple is holy, and that is what you are." (1 Corinthians 3:16 - 17)

THE PEOPLE OF THE BODY OF CHRIST TOGETHER
ARE THE HOUSE OF PRAYER

> And what agreement does the temple of God have with idols? For we are the temple of the living God, as God said: I will dwell and walk among them, and I will be their God, and they will be my people. Therefore, come out from among them and be separate, says the Lord; do not

> touch any unclean thing, and I will welcome you. And I will be a Father to you, and you will be sons and daughters to me, says the Lord Almighty. (2 Corinthians 6:16 - 18)

> So, then, you are no longer foreigners and strangers, but fellow citizens with the saints, and members of God's household, built on the foundation of the apostles and prophets, with Christ Jesus himself as the cornerstone. In him the whole building, being put together, grows into a holy temple in the Lord. In him you are also being built together for God's dwelling in the Spirit. (Ephesians 2:19 - 22)

"So Peter was kept in prison, but the church was praying fervently to God for him." (Acts 12:5) *Who* was praying for Peter? Who is the church? Where are they praying? "As soon as he [Peter] realized this, he went to the house of Mary, the mother of John who was called Mark, where many had assembled and were praying." (Acts 12:12) The church is assembled believers in the home of a family of believers. Wow! These believers are demonstrating a vibrant House of Prayer!

> As you come to him, a living stone—rejected by people but chosen and honored by God—you yourselves, as living stones, a spiritual house, are being built to be a holy priesthood to offer spiritual sacrifices acceptable to God through Jesus Christ. (1 Peter 2:4 - 5)

Where Jesus Is

We assemble in the name of Jesus when we come together as believers. "For where two or three are gathered together in my name, I [Jesus] am there among them." (Matthew 18:20)

The House of Prayer is not a building. The House of Prayer is wherever Jesus' believers gather.

> They are to make a sanctuary for me so that I may dwell among them. You must make it according to all that I show you—the pattern of the tabernacle as well as the pattern of all its furnishings. (Exodus 25:8 - 9)

"A copy and shadow of the heavenly things, as Moses was warned when he was about to complete the tabernacle. For God said, Be careful that you make everything according to the pattern that was shown to you on the mountain." (Hebrews 8:5) God gives Moses the exact pattern for the tabernacle and everything in it. The tabernacle is to be a physical representation of a heavenly center of worship.

"This was the dedication gift from the leaders of Israel for the altar when it was anointed: twelve silver dishes, twelve silver basins, and twelve gold bowls .... The twelve gold bowls full of incense each weighed four ounces measured by the standard sanctuary shekel" (Numbers 7:84 - 86). The utensils and bowls that God prescribes for the altar in the tabernacle include "twelve gold bowls full of incense." The prayers of the saints are ever before the throne of the Lamb of God (Revelation 5:8 - 9). Golden bowls of incense represent the prayers from faith-filled believers. Can you picture every gathering of believers praying kingdom-minded prayers in one accord? They saturate the soil around them with fervent prayers. This is a glimpse of heaven! The Lamb is glorified as He answers each treasured prayer.

> And I heard a loud voice from the throne, saying, "Behold, the tabernacle of God is among men, and He will dwell among them, and they shall be His people, and God Himself will be among them, and He will wipe away every tear from their eyes; and there will no longer be any death; there will no longer be any mourning, or crying, or pain; the first things have passed away." (Revelation 21:3 - 4 NASB)

Every family, every small group, every gathering of believing disciples of Jesus is sending up fragrant incense before the Lamb of God. This is a prayer revival.

Group Review and Unified Prayer Guide

Chapter 2: Foundation

INSTRUCTIONS:

- Read through the chapter review together.
- Please reserve ample time at the end of your gathering for unhurried Unified Prayer (15-30 minutes suggested).

Chapter Review

What is Alone Prayer?

Alone Prayer is time alone with God. Through intimate time with the Lord in His word and in prayer He adjusts our desires to conform with His will.

When we give Him our undivided attention it shows the high value we place on the words of Jesus as we sit at His feet to be taught by Him.

What is Unified Prayer?

Unified Prayer is a group of believers addressing God together in prayer. In Unified Prayer we interact with each other in conversation with the Lord.

The miracle of Unified Prayer is that many voices come together as one before the Lord.

What is the House of Prayer?

The House of Prayer is any place where faith-filled believers in Jesus are gathered together. The practice of prayer is the essential unifying action of these believers.

In this House of Prayer we honor the Father by coming to Him first of all with words of praise. God receives our prayers as the pleasing aroma of incense before His throne. The spiritual sacrifice we bring is our whole self in humble servitude to our Lord. The House of Prayer is a sacred place, so we must stand guard against anything that would interfere with its primary purpose of prayer.

Is the House of Prayer a building?

No, the House of Prayer is not a building. The people of the body of Christ who are gathered together are the House of Prayer.

We come together in the name of Jesus. Every small and large gathering of disciples of Jesus who pray in one accord are forming the structure of the House of Prayer.

Let's Talk About It

INSTRUCTIONS:

- Read each Scripture.
- Use the accompanying question to discuss how the Scripture relates to prayer.

"Yet he [Jesus] often withdrew to deserted places and prayed." (Luke 5:16)

Why do you think Jesus went to deserted or wilderness places to pray?

____

"Devote yourselves to prayer; stay alert in it with thanksgiving. At the same time, pray also for us that God may open a door to us for the word, to speak the mystery of Christ, for which I am in chains, so that I may make it known as I should." (Colossians 4:2 - 4)

Give examples of prayer requests that align with God's will. What reasons can you give to join in Unified Prayer for these kingdom-minded requests?

"He told those who were selling doves, 'Get these things out of here! Stop turning my Father's house into a marketplace!' And his disciples remembered that it is written: 'Zeal for your house will consume me.'" (John 2:16 - 17) "It is written, My house will be called a house of prayer" (Matthew 21:13).

Why does Jesus want prayer in His Father's house? What are some things that interfere with making prayer primary among gathered believers?

Let's Talk About It More (as time allows)

"Jesus entered a certain village where a woman named Martha welcomed him as a guest. She had a sister named Mary, who sat at the Lord's feet and listened to what he said. But Martha was distracted with all the preparations she had to make, so she came up to him and said, 'Lord, don't you care that my sister has left me to do all the work alone? Tell her to help me.' But the Lord answered her, 'Martha, Martha, you are worried and troubled about many things, but one thing is needed. Mary has chosen the best part; it will not be taken away from her.'" (Luke 10:38 - 42 NET)

What is the difference between welcoming Jesus as guest and attending to Jesus as Lord? What do you need to relinquish to be able to sit at Jesus' feet?

"The trumpeters and singers joined together to praise and thank the LORD with one voice. They raised their voices, accompanied by trumpets, cymbals, and musical instruments, in praise to the LORD: For he is good; his faithful love endures forever. The temple, the LORD's temple, was filled with a cloud. And because of the cloud, the priests were not able to continue ministering, for the glory of the LORD filled God's temple." (2 Chronicles 5:13 - 14)

The miracle of Unified Prayer is that many voices become one. What makes many voices become one voice?

"They all were continually united in prayer, along with the women, including Mary the mother of Jesus, and his brothers." (Acts 1:14)

In what way was prayer a unifying action in the early church? How might unity be strengthened among believers of today by praying together whenever we are together?

"Don't you yourselves know that you are God's temple and that the Spirit of God lives in you? If anyone destroys God's temple, God will destroy him; for God's temple is holy, and that is what you are." (1 Corinthians 3:16 - 17)

What is the House of Prayer? Where is the House of Prayer? Who is the House of Prayer?

"So Peter was kept in prison, but the church was praying fervently to God for him. ... As soon as he [Peter] realized this, he went to the house of Mary, the mother of John who was called Mark, where many had assembled and were praying." (Acts 12:5, 12)

Who is "the church" in these verses? Why do you think these believers assembled together to pray instead of just praying separately in their own homes?

Unified Prayer Building Blocks

Together:
Pray short simple prayers from the heart. Include all who want to participate.

Family:
This is a prayer conversation. Take turns. Pray one subject at a time. Listen attentively.

Unity:
Support each other with your prayers. Expound on each prayer as the Holy Spirit leads.

Let's Pray Now!

2 Foundation

Unified Prayer Guide:

INSTRUCTIONS:

- Talk through this guide together.
- Pray, implementing what you have learned.

First Step.

Talk with each other about what you want to see God do in your community. Each person writes down one topic that comes up in the conversation about which they personally care deeply. For example, "Strengthen Christian teachers in public schools." "Set free those enslaved by addiction." "Send the gospel to people with no hope."

____

Spend five minutes in Alone Prayer, with everyone remaining in place. Individually, quietly ask the Lord to draw you near to Himself. Commit your prayer habits to Him.

Next Step.

Transition to join each other in Unified Prayer. Start by taking turns saying short statements of praise to honor the Lord. For example, "Lord, You are holy." "Lord, we honor You as Creator." Continue long enough for everyone to have an opportunity to offer praise.

One person steps out and prays a short statement about the topic he or she has written down. Others take turns to express agreement with the prayer. Make it a prayer conversation with each other and the Lord.

For example, Mark: *Lord, please put godly men in our community who will nurture our boys in the ways of the Lord.* Stephen: *We ask You, Lord, to show us how to instill godly virtues in our boys at a young age.* Valerie: *Yes, Lord, would you send us men who are spiritually mature to help guide our young men to be faithful to you?*

When there is a pause, someone else steps out and prays a short statement about a topic to the Lord, and others in the group speak prayers that agree.

Continue saturating each spoken request with prayer.

Concluding Step.

When you sense that everyone has had their say in the prayer conversation, take a moment to be still in the presence of the Lord.

Anyone in the group may offer a simple concluding sentence to the prayer, such as, "Thank You, Lord, for hearing our prayers. In Jesus' name we pray, Amen."

3. Framework

UNITY IS ENHANCED when we seek the kingdom of God together with kingdom-minded prayers. As we pray together often, our hearts are woven together into cloth that will not easily unravel. When we understand the value of praying together, we give Unified Prayer first place.

> We always thank God for all of you, making mention of you constantly in our prayers. We recall, in the presence of our God and Father, your work produced by faith, your labor motivated by love, and your endurance inspired by hope in our Lord Jesus Christ. (1 Thessalonians 1:2 - 3)

The traditional Swedish weaving loom is a large wooden structure that is designed to produce high-quality woven cloth. I regularly weave on this type of loom. To dress the loom for a new project I secure the lengthwise warp threads from the warp beam at the back to the cloth beam at the front. Then I connect horizontal pivoting lamms (wooden bars) to a series of paired shafts (more wooden bars) with a series of cords. I use more cords to attach several foot treadles to the system. Finally, the loom is dressed and ready to weave. With joyful expectation I pick up a shuttle that will carry the first weft thread across the warp. My foot depresses a treadle and something amazing happens! Threads and wooden pieces and the whole assortment of cords all harmonize, moving here and there at once.

Each part moves into position for a singular purpose—to open a pathway through the warp threads. With a flick of the wrist, I propel the shuttle and it soars straight through that pathway across the warp to be caught by my other hand. When all the parts synchronize as designed, the weaving loom is a precision instrument that carries out my plans as a weaver. The result is newly woven cloth.

This is a picture of the way united prayer works. Voices from an array of believers, each essential, harmonize for one purpose—to open a pathway for God's will to be accomplished on earth. Unified Prayer is a precision instrument that carries out the plans of our Grand Weaver. He is creating the fabric of new lives in Christ with threads of faith, love, and hope woven throughout.

> Now there are different gifts, but the same Spirit. There are different ministries, but the same Lord. And there are different activities, but the same God works all of them in each person. A manifestation of the Spirit is given to each person for the common good. (1 Corinthians 12:4 - 7)

Consider the following concepts as tools that are crafted specifically for service in the House of Prayer: Seek the Kingdom of God Together, Pray Together Often, and Give Unified Prayer First Place.

SEEK THE KINGDOM OF GOD TOGETHER

SEEKING THE KINGDOM OF GOD together is a tool that gives us a focal point for the subject of every prayer.

What is the subject of our prayers? Seek the kingdom of God. "It is necessary for me [Jesus] to proclaim the good news about the kingdom of God ... because I was sent for this purpose." (Luke 4:43)

Kingdom-minded Prayers

Pray kingdom-minded prayers. This emphasis changes how we pray and what we pray for. What does it mean to be kingdom-minded? It means having God's kingdom in mind. "He has rescued us from the domain of darkness and transferred us into the kingdom of the Son he loves. In him we have redemption, the forgiveness of sins." (Colossians 1:13 - 14) Jesus has this to say about God's kingdom: "Repent, for the kingdom of heaven is near!" (Matthew 4:17 NET) "Pray like this: Our Father in heaven, your name be honored as holy. Your kingdom come. Your will be done on earth as it is in heaven." (Matthew 6:9 - 10) "But seek first the kingdom of God and his righteousness" (Matthew 6:33). "Truly I tell you, unless someone is born again, he cannot see the kingdom of God." (John 3:3)

Jesus shed His blood to purchase souls for God's kingdom. This demonstrates to us the importance of being kingdom minded!

> And they sang a new song: You are worthy to take the scroll and to open its seals, because you were slaughtered, and you purchased people for God by your blood from every tribe and language and people and nation. You made them a kingdom and priests to our God, and they will reign on the earth. (Revelation 5:9 - 10)

God provides the way of salvation and knowledge of the truth of the gospel. Kingdom-minded prayers show this focus by making a direct connection between the need at hand and God's kingdom. The need may be a troubling circumstance, a friend who does not know Christ, or a simple request for provision. Whatever the need, we can bring it into prayer with a focus on God's kingdom, where His will takes precedence.

> First of all, then, I urge that requests, prayers, intercessions, and thanks be offered on behalf of all people, even for kings and all who are in authority, that we may lead a peaceful and quiet life in all godliness and dignity. Such prayer for all is good and welcomed before God our Savior, since he wants all people to be saved and to come to a knowledge of the truth. (1 Timothy 2:1 - 4 NET)

Our prayers are a lifeline for those who are in rebellion to God. We are standing in the gap. We are calling on God to reach the lost. We are asking the Lord of the harvest to send laborers into His harvest. We must not neglect this responsibility that the Lord has given us. No one will take your place for this essential task. Your prayers make a difference for those you pray for. There may be no one else crying out to God for that one lost soul that you know. You're it.

"So he said he would have destroyed them—if Moses his chosen one had not stood before him in the breach to turn his wrath away from destroying them." (Psalm 106:23) "I looked for a man from among them who would repair the wall and stand in the gap before me on behalf of the land, so that I would not destroy it, but I found no one." (Ezekiel 22:30 NET) Let each of us be found by God as that one who is standing in the gap. The kingdom of God is directly related to God's desire to bring people to Himself. Jesus gave His disciples a vivid word picture in this regard, relating it to their personal experience with fishing.

> When he [Jesus] had finished speaking, he said to Simon, "Put out into deep water and let down your nets for a catch." "Master," Simon replied, "we've worked hard all night long and caught nothing. But if you say so, I'll let down the nets." (Luke 5:4 - 5)

Think of Unified Prayer as the beginning act of working together to lower your nets for an overflowing catch of fish. The fish represent souls. You are praying for the souls of people to be caught in this spiritual net and brought to Jesus. "'Don't be afraid,' Jesus told Simon. 'From now on you will be catching people.' Then they brought the boats to land, left everything, and followed him." (Luke 5:10 - 11)

Relationship with God

Throughout Matthew 6 Jesus teaches about relationship with the Father and public vs. secret rewards. He shows a contrast between earthly-minded religious activities and those same activities with kingdom-minded motives. How you give in private, pray in private, and fast in private shows the truth of your relationship with God. "Whenever you pray, you must not be like the hypocrites, because they love to pray standing in the synagogues and on the street corners to be seen by people ... But when you pray, go into your private room, shut your door, and pray to your Father who is in secret. And your Father who sees in secret will reward you. When you pray, don't babble ... because your Father knows the things you need before you ask him." (Matthew 6:5 - 8)

It is easy to slip into self-centered prayers where our aim is to "fix" current circumstances. We forget the kingship of the One with whom we are speaking, and we ask for earthly-minded solutions to temporal problems. "Lord, please take care of this, and this, and this. Remove the difficulty, satisfy my wants, and help all my friends. And Lord, show me how Your purposes fit into my plans." Where's the Father-child relationship? Where's the servant bowing to his King?

Kingdom-minded prayers are those that grow out of our relationship with the Father. Requests that come from this vital relationship begin with the desire for His will to be accomplished. Speak prayers worthy of the King and His kingdom. Pray that God's will be done here.

Our prayers must rise higher than our self-centered concerns. "Yet, there is a higher way to pray. By that, I mean that a self-centered prayer is a low prayer, and prayer from an unselfish motive is a high prayer. Rather than our prayer lives being filled with requests for ourselves, what if they issued from a deep desire to see God glorified?" These thoughts from my son Samuel's booklet, *The 3 Keys of Availing Prayer*, remind us of the true purpose of prayer—that God's will be done, not for our temporal objectives, but for His glory.[5]

Instead of my will be done, pray Thy will be done. What does Jesus tell us to seek? And not to seek? "And do not seek what you will eat and what you will drink, and do not keep worrying. For all these things the nations of the world eagerly seek; but your Father knows that you need these things. But seek His kingdom, and these things will be added to you. Do not be afraid, little flock, for your Father has chosen gladly to give you the kingdom." (Luke 12:29 - 32 NASB)

Prayer is not us making demands on God. Nor is it a way for us to have our wishes fulfilled. Prayer is coming to God open-handed to receive what He wants to give. S. D. Gordon says it best: "The roots of prayer lie down in oneness of purpose. God up yonder, His Victor-Son by His side, and a man down here, in such sympathetic touch that God can think His thoughts over in this man's mind, and have His desires repeated upon the earth as this man's prayer."[6]

Instead of requesting something that will make my life, or someone else's life, easier, better, happier, we are interested in connecting those needs to the Father's will regarding His kingdom.

God's Will

How does God's will relate to the need at hand? What is the spiritual need? Think about how God's will goes beyond meeting a physical need. Because of my relationship with God, I want my prayer to be in line with

His will. This desire for God's will to be accomplished is the key to praying kingdom-minded prayers. God reveals His will in His word and confirms it by the Holy Spirit. "'Thy will be done.' Every true prayer comes under those four words."[7]

THE DESIRE FOR GOD'S WILL IS THE KEY TO PRAYING KINGDOM-MINDED PRAYERS

> Make your ways known to me, LORD; teach me your paths. Guide me in your truth and teach me, for you are the God of my salvation; I wait for you all day long. (Psalm 25:4 - 5)

Frame your prayer with God's purposes in mind. Instead of, "Keep my child from getting in trouble," and, "Give my friend a job," and, "Stop my friend from falling to temptation," and "Help me get more done today," consider these kingdom-minded alternatives:

"Lord, bring my child out of his wayward path so that he will honor You with his decisions."

"Lord, for my sister in Christ who just lost her job, please reposition her where she will be able to use the gifts You have created in her, for Your glory."

"Father, dress my friend in Your full armor so he can remain faithful in Christ and stand firm against temptations from the enemy."

"Lord, would you direct me to see how to use my time today? I want to be available to speak the gospel with those You put in my path."

Right Desires

Let godly desires lead your prayers. Beware of praying from your fears. Fear keeps our eyes on the problem. Praying from right desires helps keep our eyes on Jesus to align with God's will through faith. "What the wicked dreads will come to him, but what the righteous desire will be given to them." (Proverbs 10:24) "Take delight in the LORD, and he will give you your heart's desires." (Psalm 37:4)

Our religious prayers have no effect on God when we live in rebellion to His ways. He chooses not to listen.

> When you spread out your hands in prayer, I will refuse to look at you; even if you offer countless prayers, I will not listen. Your hands are covered with blood. "Wash yourselves. Cleanse yourselves. Remove your evil deeds from my sight. Stop doing evil." (Isaiah 1:15 - 16)

He waits for prayers that serve to accomplish His will. If we are not interested in His will, why should we expect Him to answer our prayers? "Whatever you ask in my name, I will do it so that the Father may be glorified in the Son. If you ask me anything in my name, I will do it. If you love me, you will keep my commands." (John 14:13 - 15)

God's kingdom is where God has the rightful rule in a person's life. When God's rightful rule is in place in our lives, our needs are met. Right desires are granted. "Your kingdom come. Your will be done on earth as it is in heaven." (Matthew 6:10) "For the Gentiles eagerly seek all these things, and Your heavenly Father knows that You need them. But seek first the kingdom of God and His righteousness, and all these things will be provided for You." (Matthew 6:32 - 33)

Pursuit of His kingdom and His righteousness is the heart of kingdom-minded prayers.

PRAY TOGETHER OFTEN

PRAYING TOGETHER OFTEN is a tool that turns every gathering of believers into an opportunity for meaningful prayer.

What is the frequency of our prayers? Pray together often. "They devoted themselves to the apostles' teaching, to the fellowship, to the breaking of bread, and to prayer." (Acts 2:42) When believers are together, we have the unparalleled privilege of coming to the Father to saturate needs in united prayer. When together, pray together!

WHEN TOGETHER, PRAY TOGETHER!

Opportunity

Have you noticed how often the apostle Paul mentions his prayers, and how frequently he requests prayer from others? His letters to churches presume that believers are praying together. "On the Sabbath day we went outside the city gate by the river, where we expected to find a place of prayer. We sat down and spoke to the women gathered there." (Acts 16:13)

Oh, that more people would pray together more often! Let us open our eyes to see how available we can be to pray. Stay alert with intentional readiness. We must not overlook any opportunity we have to raise our faith in prayer with other believers.

"My goal is that their hearts, having been knit together in love, may be encouraged, and that they may have all the riches that assurance brings in their understanding of the knowledge of the mystery of God, namely, Christ, in whom are hidden all the treasures of wisdom and knowledge." (Colossians 2:2 - 3 NET) We have a spiritual gold mine in our midst. Are there other pursuits more valuable than this? Let us not only tap the surface, let us dig deep for the treasures that are found only in this holy ground of meeting together with Christ. “Devote yourselves to prayer; stay alert in it with thanksgiving.” (Colossians 4:2) In *With Christ in the School of Prayer*, Andrew Murray asks, “Who can say what power a Church could develop and exercise, if it gave itself to the work of prayer day and night for the coming of the kingdom, for God’s power on His servants and His word, for the glorifying of God in the salvation of souls?”[8]

Increased Faith

When we pray together, it increases our faith. We hear faith that is spoken in someone else’s words. This benefits each person in the group. Vibrancy of faith is contagious, and everyone grows in confidence as a result. “This is the confidence we have before him: If we ask anything according to his will, he hears us. And if we know that he hears whatever we ask, we know that we have what we have asked of him.” (1 John 5:14 - 15)

> Don’t worry about anything, but in everything, through prayer and petition with thanksgiving, present your requests to God. And the peace of God, which surpasses all understanding, will guard your hearts and minds in Christ Jesus. (Philippians 4:6 - 7)

GIVE UNIFIED PRAYER FIRST PLACE

GIVING UNIFIED PRAYER FIRST PLACE is a tool that places high value on prayer, which also effectively opens more time for Unified Prayer.

What is the worth of our prayers? Give Unified Prayer first place. “‘My food is to do the will of him who sent me and to finish his work,’ Jesus told them. ‘Don’t you say, “There are still four more months, and then comes the harvest”? Listen to what I’m telling you: Open your eyes and look at the fields, because they are ready for harvest.’” (John 4:34 - 35)

Priority

When we see prayer as our first option, we allow the Holy Spirit to take the stage—front and center—not backstage. We give first place to things that we value most. "Some trust in chariots and some in horses, but we trust in the name of the Lord our God." (Psalm 20:7 ESV) Do we understand the crucial nature of prayer? Are we vibrant and unstoppable, like the church we see in the book of Acts? "Has the Lord changed? Has the Spirit stopped His ministry? Has Jesus stopped willing that none should perish (2 Peter 3:9)?," asks Samuel Isenhower in *The 3 Keys of Availing Prayer*.[9]

Prioritizing prayer means making ample time for unhurried Unified Prayer. For example, Unified Prayer at the beginning of a gathering opens the possibility of an extended prayer time. Another approach is to preserve time at the end of a meeting. Intentionally set apart time for unhurried Unified Prayer. We show the high value of praying together when we purposely make more than enough time for it. Priority status shows that we understand the urgency of the times we live in, and that we have been called to be unstoppable in prayer.

GIVE UNIFIED PRAYER FIRST PLACE
BY MAKING AMPLE TIME

An advantage of praying together at the start is that it prevents rushed praying at the end. "We're out of time. I'll pray a quick prayer to close our time together." Have you closed a small group time, Sunday School class, or Bible study with those words? Starting with Unified Prayer has the added benefit of bringing us into the Lord's presence to till the soil for anything else He wants to plant in us during our time together. Prayer first has the potential to turn our whole time together into a Holy Spirit-led prayer meeting. Are we hungry for that? If so, we will see God intervene in powerful ways, where people leave refreshed, with burdens lifted. We may see the Holy Spirit change our agenda and guide us in a different direction than we had planned. When this happens, everyone gets to experience the transforming power of the presence of the Lord.

Praying together at the end of our fellowship has the positive effect of watering the soil of our hearts where the Lord has planted truth through teaching, conversation, and ministry. This is when hearts and minds are ripe for true repentance, restoration, and renewal as we pray in unity with each other.

In short, let every time we meet include Unified Prayer where we are doing more than sprinkling the soil just enough to dampen the top layer. Let us invest time together into prayers that deeply saturate the soil.

Pray Now

When there is a need, don't wait. Pray together now. Let's be the church family that prays together earnestly, like Peter's friends who are praying for him in a crisis. Peter is in prison with a likely death sentence, awaiting trial before Herod. This community of believers has recently lost a dear friend who was martyred for his faith. Nothing can make them hesitate to pray together now. "So Peter was kept in prison, but those in the church were earnestly praying to God for him. On that very night before Herod was going to bring him out for trial, Peter was sleeping between two soldiers, bound with two chains, while guards in front of the door were keeping watch over the prison. Suddenly an angel of the Lord appeared, and a light shone in the prison cell. He struck Peter on the side and woke him up, saying, 'Get up quickly!' And the chains fell off Peter's wrists." (Acts 12:5 - 7 NET)

Peter's friends who pray together make an immeasurable investment in the future of the gospel through the life of Peter the apostle. Aren't we glad someone said, "Let's pray now!"?

USE BUILDING BLOCKS FOR PRAYING TOGETHER

Effectiveness

THREE BUILDING BLOCKS strengthen the effectiveness of our Unified Prayers.

1. Together: Everyone contributes. *No insignificant voice.*
2. Family: Family conversation. *The practice of listening.*
3. Unity: One heart and mind. *We are in this together.*

These elements lead us into unity of faith.

Unity

Be of the same mind, have the same love, be united in spirit, have one purpose. All these things are accomplished in Unified Prayer. "Therefore, if there is any encouragement in Christ, any comfort provided by love, any fellowship in the Spirit, any affection or mercy, complete my joy and be of the same mind, by having the same love, being united in spirit, and having one purpose." (Philippians 2:1 - 2 NET)

Let's pray!

Group Review and Unified Prayer Guide

Chapter 3: Framework

INSTRUCTIONS:

- Read through the chapter review together.
- Please reserve ample time at the end of your gathering for unhurried Unified Prayer (15-30 minutes suggested).

Chapter Review

Seek the kingdom of God together.

We seek the kingdom of God together by praying kingdom-minded prayers. This emphasis changes how we pray and what we pray for, so that we connect every need to God's will.

We want our prayers to grow out of our relationship with the Father. Requests that come from this vital relationship begin with the desire for His will to be accomplished. God's will goes beyond meeting a physical need, so we frame our prayers with God's purposes in mind. Our desires will affect our prayers, so we must allow the Lord to adjust our desires to align with His will. He answers those whose desire it is for His will to be done.

Pray together often.

Every gathering of believers holds promise for meaningful prayer. We must not overlook any opportunity we have to raise our faith in prayer with other believers.

Our faith increases as we hear each other pray. Your vibrant faith encourages me, and my prayers of faith encourage you.

Give Unified Prayer first place.

Show the high value of Unified Prayer by making it a priority. Giving Unified Prayer first place means making ample time for unhurried Unified Prayer.

We make it a priority by investing time in prayer at the beginning of a gathering, or by planning for ample time in prayer before the end of our fellowship together. Be ready for times when there is an imminent need for prayer. Be the one to say, "Let's pray together now!"

Let's Talk About It

INSTRUCTIONS:

- Read each Scripture.
- Use the accompanying question to discuss how the Scripture relates to prayer.

"It is necessary for me [Jesus] to proclaim the good news about the kingdom of God ... because I was sent for this purpose. (Luke 4:43) Pray like this: Our Father in heaven, your name be honored as holy. Your kingdom come. Your will be done on earth as it is in heaven. ...But seek first the kingdom of God and his righteousness" (Matthew 6:9 - 10, 33).

What is the difference between a kingdom-minded prayer and an earthly-minded prayer? How does a kingdom-minded emphasis change how we pray and what we pray for?

"Devote yourselves to prayer; stay alert in it with thanksgiving." (Colossians 4:2)

What actions show that we are devoted to something?

"So Peter was kept in prison, but those in the church were earnestly praying to God for him. On that very night before Herod was going to bring him out for trial, Peter was sleeping between two soldiers, bound with two chains, while guards in front of the door were keeping watch over the prison. Suddenly an angel of the Lord appeared, and a light shone in the prison cell. He struck Peter on the side and woke him up, saying, 'Get up quickly!' And the chains fell off Peter's wrists." (Acts 12:5 - 7 NET)

What might we have missed if Peter's church family had not taken time to pray for him when they did? What might future generations miss if we neglect Unified Prayer today?

Let's Talk About It More (as time allows)

"Make your ways known to me, Lord; teach me your paths. Guide me in your truth and teach me, for you are the God of my salvation; I wait for you all day long." (Psalm 25:4 - 5)

How does God's will go beyond meeting a physical need? Give an example of a kingdom-minded prayer—for a friend who is looking for a job; for a student deciding where to go to college; for a relative enduring long-term illness.

"Don't worry about anything, but in everything, through prayer and petition with thanksgiving, present your requests to God. And the peace of God, which surpasses all understanding, will guard your hearts and minds in Christ Jesus." (Philippians 4:6 - 7)

How does prayer reduce worries and increase faith? In what way does Unified Prayer put a peace guard over our hearts and minds in Christ Jesus?

"Some trust in chariots and some in horses, but we trust in the name of the Lord our God." (Psalm 20:7 ESV)

What does it demonstrate when we invest ample time in Unified Prayer when we are together? What does it demonstrate if we do not allow ample time for Unified Prayer?

Unified Prayer Building Blocks

Together:
Pray short simple prayers from the heart. Include all who want to participate.

Family:
This is a prayer conversation. Take turns. Pray one subject at a time. Listen attentively.

Unity:
Support each other with your prayers. Expound on each prayer as the Holy Spirit leads.

Let's Pray Now!

3 Framework

Unified Prayer Guide:

INSTRUCTIONS:

- Talk through this guide together.
- Pray, implementing what you have learned.

First Step.

Each person writes down the name of someone whom they want Jesus to reach. For example, a family member, a co-worker, or a neighbor.

____

Have a group conversation about what each of you want to ask God to do in people's lives. No gossip allowed. Focus on what God can do.

Next Step.

Start by taking turns praying short statements of praise to honor the Lord's name. For example, "Lord, You are the Good Shepherd." "Jesus, You are the King of Kings and Lord of Lords. We worship You." Continue until everyone is finished offering words of praise.

One person steps out and prays for the individual whose name he or she has written down. Others take turns to express agreement with the prayer. Make it a prayer conversation with each other and the Lord.

For example, Bill: *Lord, please open the door for my friend to hear the gospel.* Addie: *Yes, Lord, we ask that You would prepare Bill's friend to receive Your word.* Jack: *We ask that you transfer Bill's friend out of darkness into your kingdom of light.*

When there is a pause, someone else steps out and prays for another individual. Continue the prayer conversation as long as time allows.

Continue saturating each spoken request with prayer.

Concluding Step.

When you sense that everyone has had their say in the prayer conversation, take a moment to be still in the presence of the Lord.

Anyone in the group may offer a simple concluding sentence to the prayer, such as, "Thank You, Lord, for hearing our prayer. In Jesus' name we pray, Amen."

Priority of Prayer

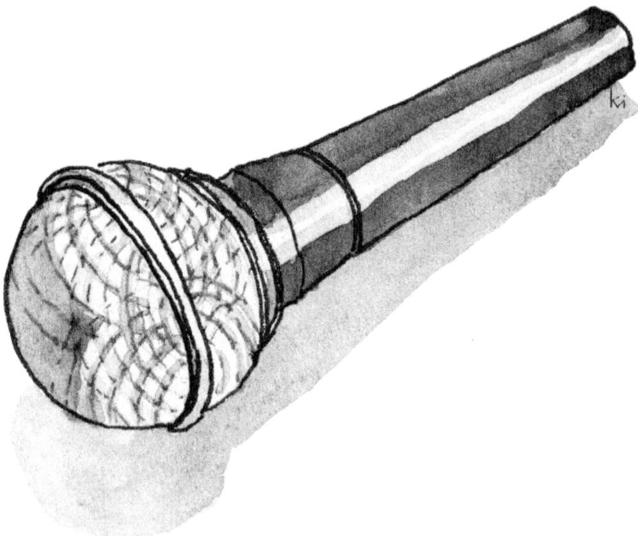

No Insignificant Voice

4. Together

Everyone contributes. *No insignificant voice.*

WE ARE KNIT TOGETHER

Spiritual Growth

IN PAUL'S LETTER TO THE COLOSSIANS he tells them that his goal is that their hearts may be encouraged. His prayer is that they would be knit together in love. Believers are knit together in the body of Christ for the purpose of mutual spiritual growth, with the aim of serving God's kingdom. "For I want you to know how great a struggle I have for you, and for those in Laodicea, and for those who have not met me face to face. My goal is that their hearts, having been knit together in love, may be encouraged, and that they may have all the riches that assurance brings in their understanding of the knowledge of the mystery of God, namely, Christ, in whom are hidden all the treasures of wisdom and knowledge." (Colossians 2:1 - 3 NET)

We must hold on to Christ our head. Individually and corporately, we depend on Christ as we grow with God-blessed spiritual growth. The whole body of Christ is supported and knit together through Christ, our head. "Hold on to the head [Christ], from whom the whole body, nourished and held together by its ligaments and tendons, grows with growth from God." (Colossians 2:19)

We are knit together as we pursue God's kingdom together, encouraging each other to walk in faithfulness to the Lord.

"Flee from youthful passions, and pursue righteousness, faith, love, and peace, along with those who call on the Lord from a pure heart." (2 Timothy 2:22) As Paul writes to Timothy, we, too, must pursue godly virtues "along with those" in our community of fellow Christ followers. This community is strong because we "call on the Lord from a pure heart" together. We focus on God's kingdom and grow with each other through Unified Prayer. Our hearts are knit together in love as we petition God to accomplish His will through our prayers.

LOVE KNITS US TOGETHER
IN THE BODY OF CHRIST

Faith Out Loud

When we pray out loud together we put words to our faith that reach God's ears. In the gospel accounts we read many times that Jesus is interested in hearing people express their faith. Jesus sometimes asks a question that helps someone express his faith out loud. Jesus searches for faith in people.

> Jesus stopped and commanded that he [a blind man] be brought to him. When he came closer, he asked him, "What do you want me to do for you?" "Lord," he said, "I want to see." "Receive your sight," Jesus told him. "Your faith has saved you." (Luke 18:40 - 42)

Matthew records an instance when Jesus ignites two blind men's faith with a question, which gives them an opportunity to put words to their faith. "Jesus said to them, 'Do you believe that I can do this?' They said to him, 'Yes, Lord.' Then he touched their eyes, saying, 'Let it be done for you according to your faith.' And their eyes were opened" (Matthew 9:27 - 30).

We express faith through prayer by speaking what we believe. Thinking true thoughts is important. Speaking true thoughts goes a step further and becomes an anchor for faith. The simple act of speaking can move faith from our head to our heart. "May the words of my mouth and the meditation of my heart be acceptable to you, Lord, my rock and my Redeemer." (Psalm 19:14)

The thought of my heart reveals the state of my faithfulness, and my words reveal faith that pleases the Lord. We speak what we believe. Unified Prayer combines words of believers to speak with faith to the Lord. "Since we have the same spirit of faith according to what has been written, 'I believed, and so I spoke,' we also believe, and so we also speak, knowing that he who raised the Lord Jesus will raise us also with Jesus and bring us with you into his presence." (2 Corinthians 4:13 - 14 ESV)

EVERYONE CONTRIBUTES

Jump In

THE FULLNESS OF THE BODY OF CHRIST is revealed when we participate in Unified Prayer. This is where harmony flourishes among believers. We are one body and many essential parts. We need each one of us. "For just as the body is one and has many parts, and all the parts of that body, though many, are one body—so also is Christ. For we were all baptized by one Spirit into one body—whether Jews or Greeks, whether slaves or free—and we were all given one Spirit to drink. Indeed, the body is not one part but many." (1 Corinthians 12:12 - 14)

We come together with unified hearts, praying together as one. We are able to saturate every thanksgiving, request, and godly desire with needed prayer when we all join in together. Where would we be if only certain ones of us were mature enough, outgoing enough, wise enough, strong enough, or well-spoken enough to pray? "But as it is, God has arranged each one of the parts in the body just as he wanted. And if they were all the same part, where would the body be? As it is, there are many parts, but one body ... God has put the body together, giving greater honor to the less honorable, so that there would be no division in the body, but that the members would have the same concern for each other. So if one member suffers, all the members suffer with it; if one member is honored, all the members rejoice with it." (1 Corinthians 12:18 - 26)

Think back to childhood playground days. Remember the long jump-rope, with one person at each end holding the handles to turn the rope? We take turns jumping in and jumping out. When it is your turn you watch the jump-rope, get the rhythm of it, and then jump in without breaking the rhythm. When it's the next person's turn you jump out. Jump in, jump out, pay attention, be ready, jump in, jump out.

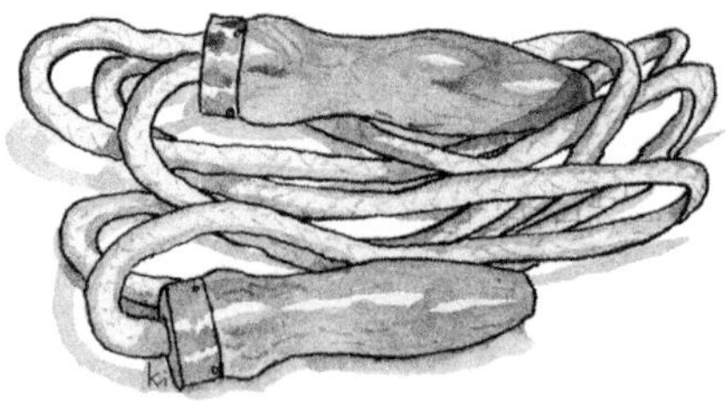

PRAY TOGETHER WITH READINESS,
TAKING TURNS, STAYING IN THE RHYTHM OF
CONVERSATIONAL PRAYER

We can pray together with that kind of readiness, taking turns, staying in the rhythm of the conversational prayer at hand. Jump in, jump out. Ready to jump in to offer words as the Holy Spirit directs. Ready to jump out so the next person can add their personal words. This willingness to take turns is an indispensable concept to grasp. This one thing turns any prayer session into a beautiful demonstration of a fully functioning body of Christ, as all lean into God's will. "Now you are the body of Christ, and individual members of it." (1 Corinthians 12:27)

Accept the Invitation

Everyone is invited to participate. We pray together with back-and-forth interaction among all who accept the invitation to join in. The Spirit of God is the One who gives each of us the grace to do what we are not strong enough to do on our own. "You, however, are not in the flesh, but in the Spirit, if indeed the Spirit of God lives in you ... And if the Spirit of him who raised Jesus from the dead lives in you, then he who raised Christ from the dead will also bring your mortal bodies to life through his Spirit who lives in you." (Romans 8:9 - 11)

Each individual presses in to listen, voice agreement, and initiate requests as the Holy Spirit brings thoughts to express in prayer. By His overflowing grace we have everything we need to be able to participate in Unified Prayer. "And God is able to make every grace overflow to you, so that in every way, always having everything you need, you may excel in every good work." (2 Corinthians 9:8)

Every believer has something to contribute. Praying out loud is not easy for some, but it is a worthwhile challenge. We have been given a direct communication line with our heavenly Father. Those who have the Spirit of God are able to pray. The Holy Spirit directs the heart of prayer in them. "In the same way the Spirit also helps us in our weakness, because we do not know what to pray for as we should, but the Spirit himself intercedes for us with inexpressible groanings. And he who searches our hearts knows the mind of the Spirit, because he intercedes for the saints according to the will of God." (Romans 8:26 - 27)

We sometimes think we have nothing to add. We don't know what to say. We don't know how to pray with others. We fear we might say the wrong thing. We would rather let the others in the group do the talking when it comes to prayer. We think we have nothing to say but a few small words.

> Elisha said to her, "What can I do for you? Tell me, what do you have in the house?" She answered, "Your servant has nothing in the house except a small jar of olive oil." He said, "Go and ask all your neighbors for empty containers. Get as many as you can. Go and close the door behind you and your sons. Pour the olive oil into all the containers; set aside each one when you have filled it." So she left him and closed the door behind her and her sons. As they were bringing the containers to her, she was pouring the olive oil. When the containers were full, she said to one of her sons, "Bring me another container." But he answered her, "There are no more." Then the olive oil stopped flowing. She went and told the prophet. He said, "Go, sell the olive oil. Repay your creditor, and then you and your sons can live off the rest of the profit." (2 Kings 4:2 - 7 NET)

What do you have in your house? You may have nothing except a few small words. Pour out the few words that you have and watch God fill your need. It takes faith to obey. Obedience is faith.

Voicing an earnest prayer is voicing faith, which is what Jesus seeks from us. There is no safer place to voice an earnest prayer to God than in the presence of Christ-minded believers. If the Spirit of Christ lives in you, you have everything you need to speak words in prayer with fellow believers who are also alive in Christ.

Bold Faith

Allow the Holy Spirit to lead every prayer and request. We position ourselves to receive His direction as we pray in faith together. "Pray at all times in the Spirit with every prayer and request, and stay alert with all perseverance and intercession for all the saints." (Ephesians 6:18)

Praying out loud brings the prayer of our hearts into the open and gives clarity to our thoughts. Your heart believes, and your mouth speaks what you believe. Prayer in community with other believers is a sacred place to speak what your heart believes. "One believes with the heart, resulting in righteousness, and one confesses with the mouth, resulting in salvation. For the Scripture says, 'Everyone who believes on him will not be put to shame, since there is no distinction between Jew and Greek, because the same Lord of all richly blesses all who call on him. For everyone who calls on the name of the Lord will be saved.'" (Romans 10:10 - 13)

How can we help those who are uncomfortable praying out loud with others? Let us remind each other that our prayers are important to God. Let us persuade each other that the body of Christ is strengthened in faith when we allow others to come into our prayer conversation with the Lord. Are we not each encouraged when we hear prayers of faith from fellow believers on our behalf? Likewise, your prayer encourages those who hear you pray for them.

When we are in the company of Jesus followers we can pray what is on our hearts. Jesus taught us to pray, not to impress people with our eloquent words, but to be heard by God. Our heavenly Father wants to hear our heart-felt prayers, and so do our brothers and sisters in Christ. We must make it clear that people can pray their most vulnerable requests and know that it goes no further than the prayer closet of brothers and sisters in Christ. Gossip in all its forms is forbidden. Prayer is a sacred space to pour out our hearts to the Lord. It requires a sacred trust of one another.

"For God did not give us a Spirit of fear [timidity] but of power and love and self-control." (2 Timothy 1:7 NET) Anyone can overcome the silence barrier. Someone who feels timid about praying out loud with others but wants to gain confidence can practice by praying out loud when alone. The quiet natured person can ask the Lord to give a few simple words to pray out loud in a group. Our courage increases as we obey the small steps the Lord gives us, and as we listen to others pray. Keep trusting Him to lead each of us to full participation. Keep putting yourself in the company of people who pray.

"Do not be anxious about anything. Instead, in every situation, through prayer and petition with thanksgiving, tell your requests to God. And the peace of God that surpasses all understanding will guard your hearts and minds in Christ Jesus." (Philippians 4:6 - 7 NET) Faith that is spoken is bold faith. Jesus is looking for that kind of faith. Our Lord responds to courageous faith.

Persistence

Persistence in prayer shows that we are not willing to lose heart, but that we stand firm in faith. We pray, and will continue to pray, and will keep on praying, knowing that God is hearing and answering according to His will. "Then Jesus told them a parable to show them they should always pray and not lose heart ... 'Won't God give justice to his chosen ones, who cry out to him day and night? Will he delay long to help them? I tell you, he will give them justice speedily. Nevertheless, when the Son of Man comes, will he find faith on earth?'" (Luke 18:1, 7 - 8 NET) Faith is believing that God hears us, and that He wants to hear what we have to say.

"I will stand at my watch post; I will remain stationed on the city wall. I will keep watching so I can see what he says to me and can know how I should answer when he counters my argument." (Habakkuk 2:1 NET) We stand at our watch post, and we will remain stationed. We will keep watching. Jesus is coming again. Will He find us stationed on the wall with faith? Will we be persistent in prayer?

We know that Paul and his co-laborers were men and women of prayer. Some of their prayers are written down, which give us a clear model of persistent prayer.

> This is why, since I heard about your faith in the Lord Jesus and your love for all the saints, I never stop giving thanks for you as I remember you in my prayers. I pray that the God of our Lord Jesus Christ, the glorious Father, would give you the Spirit of wisdom and revelation in the knowledge of him. I pray that the eyes of your heart may be enlightened so that you may know what is the hope of his calling, what is the wealth of his glorious inheritance in the saints, and what is the immeasurable greatness of his power toward us who believe, according to the mighty working of his strength. (Ephesians 1:15 - 19)

"In view of this, we always pray for you that our God will make you worthy of his calling, and by his power fulfill your every desire to do good and your work produced by faith, so that the name of our Lord Jesus will be glorified by you, and you by him, according to the grace of our God and the Lord Jesus Christ." (2 Thessalonians 1:11 - 12) According to Andrew Murray it is evident that Paul "counted on the prayers of these Churches to gain for him, what otherwise might not be given."[10]

When we advance the opportunity for each other to pray, we are encouraging each other's faith. Praying out loud in unity helps everyone gain even more confidence to pray out loud. This is as true for those mature in faith as it is for those new in faith.

Have the persistence to keep coming to God in Unified Prayer, earnestly crying out to Him. Don't give up. He hears you. Faith doesn't quit. Pray for the justice of God's kingdom to come, for His will to be done, especially for the most difficult circumstances. That is when we need each other to join our voices in heartfelt supplication to the Lord.

"And a widow in that town kept coming to him, saying, 'Give me justice against my adversary.'" (Luke 18:3) Always pray and do not lose heart. Keep praying; keep crying out to God. The widow had no other protection from her adversary, so she came again and again to the judge, knowing he was able to help her if he wanted to. She had faith that the judge would eventually respond. Our faith is in a righteous Judge. We keep coming to Him, knowing He is able and that He wants to make things right.

> Lord, God of my salvation, I cry out before you day and night. May my prayer reach your presence; listen to my cry. For I have had enough troubles, and my life is near Sheol. (Psalm 88:1 - 3)

God looks for those who believe Him. "The Lord looks down from heaven on the children of man, to see if there are any who understand, who seek after God." (Psalm 14:2 ESV)

Every Voice Is Essential

Teaching and instruction from a wise person is a fountain of life. Drink from it. Avoid the traps of death by saturating yourself with wise advice. What better way to soak up wisdom than to participate in prayer with someone who has an intimate relationship with Jesus? "A wise person's instruction is a fountain of life, turning people away from the snares of death." (Proverbs 13:14)

When you pray with other believers it helps you gain faith in areas where you are weak. When you pray for strength and faith you begin to let go of what you know and let God take over with what He knows. In the words of Andrew Murray, "What an unspeakable privilege this of united prayer is, and what a power it might be ... if in every Church united effectual prayer were regarded as one of the chief purposes for which they are banded together, the highest exercise of their power as a Church."[11]

We need every voice in prayer. Every member of the body serves a specific function. We each see, hear, and speak from our own perspective. I need to hear what you pray, because you bring a new perspective that ignites my faith. You need to hear what I pray, because the Lord wants to unite our hearts together. In God's kingdom there is no introvert or extrovert, shy or gregarious. We drop self labels to be one in Christ.

> As you come to him, a living stone—rejected by people but chosen and honored by God—you yourselves, as living stones, a spiritual house, are being built to be a holy priesthood to offer spiritual sacrifices acceptable to God through Jesus Christ. (1 Peter 2:4 - 5)

In Unified Prayer each person contributes as an essential member of the body. The Holy Spirit will give you or me a thought that no one else has considered. Every voice matters.

This is how we come together in the House of Prayer.

Group Review and Unified Prayer Guide

Chapter 4: Together

Chapter Review

We are knit together.

Love knits us together in the body of Christ for the purpose of mutual spiritual growth. Our hearts are united as we petition God to accomplish His will through our prayers.

Praying out loud with each other produces fertile soil for our faith to grow. The simple act of speaking can move our faith from our head to our heart. Unified Prayer gives us a way to express our faith out loud together.

Everyone contributes.

We are one body with many essential parts. Remember the long jump rope from childhood playground days? We take turns jumping in and jumping out. When it is your turn you watch the jump rope, get the rhythm of it, and then jump in. When it's the next person's turn you jump out. Jump in, jump out, pay attention. We can pray together with that kind of readiness, taking turns, staying in the rhythm of conversational prayer.

The Spirit of God has given each of us the grace to be able to accept the invitation to participate.

Someone who feels timid about praying out loud with others can gain confidence by practicing prayer out loud when alone. Even a quiet-natured person can pray a few simple words. Our courage increases as we listen to others pray and as we keep putting ourselves in the company of people who pray.

Keep persisting in Unified Prayer, especially for the most difficult circumstances. We need each other. Unified Prayer gives each person a way to contribute as an essential member of the body of Christ.

Let's Talk About It

INSTRUCTIONS:

- Read each Scripture.
- Use the accompanying question to discuss how the Scripture relates to prayer.

"For I want you to know how great a struggle I have for you, and for those in Laodicea, and for those who have not met me face to face. My goal is that their hearts, having been knit together in love, may be encouraged, and that they may have all the riches that assurance brings in their understanding of the knowledge of the mystery of God, namely, Christ, in whom are hidden all the treasures of wisdom and knowledge." (Colossians 2:1 - 3 NET)

How do we better serve God's kingdom when our hearts are knit together in love? In what ways are our hearts knit together in Unified Prayer?

"For just as the body is one and has many parts, and all the parts of that body, though many, are one body—so also is Christ. For we were all baptized by one Spirit into one body—whether Jews or Greeks, whether slaves or free—and we were all given one Spirit to drink. Indeed, the body is not one part but many. ... Now you are the body of Christ, and individual members of it." (1 Corinthians 12:12 - 14, 27)

We are one body and many essential parts. Why is every voice essential in Unified Prayer?

"For God did not give us a Spirit of fear [timidity] but of power and love and self-control." (2 Timothy 1:7 NET)

What does God not give us? What does God give us? In what way do these gifts help us speak up in Unified Prayer?

Let's Talk About It More (as time allows)

"Since we have the same spirit of faith according to what has been written, 'I believed, and so I spoke,' we also believe, and so we also speak, knowing that he who raised the Lord Jesus will raise us also with Jesus and bring us with you into his presence." (2 Corinthians 4:13 - 14 ESV)

Our words reveal faith that pleases the Lord. In what way does praying out loud in Unified Prayer help us grow in faith together?

"And God is able to make every grace overflow to you, so that in every way, always having everything you need, you may excel in every good work." (2 Corinthians 9:8)

What is needed to be able to excel in every good work? What is needed to be able to participate in the good work of Unified Prayer?

"Then Jesus told them a parable to show them they should always pray and not lose heart. ... 'Won't God give justice to his chosen ones, who cry out to him day and night? Will he delay long to help them? I tell you, he will give them justice speedily. Nevertheless, when the Son of Man comes, will he find faith on earth?'" (Luke 18:1, 7 - 8 NET)

Why does faith not lose heart? How does persistence in prayer show that we have faith?

Unified Prayer Building Blocks

Together:
Pray short simple prayers from the heart. Include all who want to participate.

Family:
This is a prayer conversation. Take turns. Pray one subject at a time. Listen attentively.

Unity:
Support each other with your prayers. Expound on each prayer as the Holy Spirit leads.

Let's Pray Now!

4 Together

Unified Prayer Guide:

INSTRUCTIONS:

- Talk through this guide together.
- Pray, implementing what you have learned.

First Step.

Each person thinks about one or two petitions that they have brought to the Lord during their Alone Prayer times this week. For example, prayer for a friend or family member, for someone in leadership, or prayer for personal decision making.

If it helps you, each person writes down the main point of their one or two petitions.

Next Step.

Start by taking turns praying short statements of praise to honor the Lord.

Quietly form small clusters of three to four people. In each small cluster, one person starts by praying for one of the petitions on his or her heart. Keep the petition short and simple so others in the group have the opportunity to engage in the prayer through the guidance of the Holy Spirit. Make it a prayer conversation with each other and the Lord.

When there is a pause, another person introduces a petition for prayer in the small cluster. Continue the prayer conversation for as long as time allows.

Concluding Step.

For the final minutes, quietly regroup to resume praying altogether.

Speak prayers of thanksgiving in a prayer conversation for what the Lord is doing among you.

When you sense that everyone has had their say in the prayer conversation, take a moment to be still in the presence of the Lord.

Anyone in the group may offer a simple concluding sentence to the prayer, such as, "Thank You, Lord, for hearing our prayers. In Jesus' name we pray, Amen."

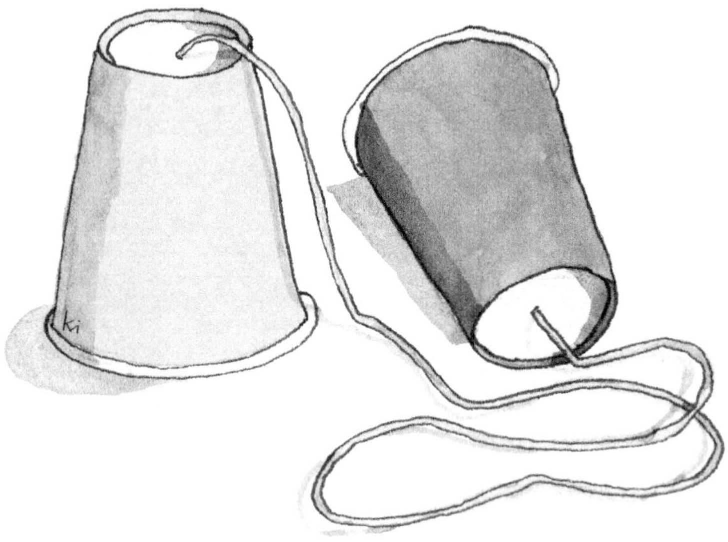

The Practice of Listening

5. Family

Family conversation. *The practice of listening.*

PRAYER IS A CONVERSATION

One Conversation

FOLD YOUR HANDS, BOW YOUR HEAD, close your eyes. Maybe you learned this prayer posture as a child. When we read prayers of gathered believers in the book of Acts, do we assume people are separately whispering their prayers with heads bowed and eyes closed? "After they [Peter and John] were released, they went to their own people and reported everything the chief priests and the elders had said to them. When they heard this, they raised their voices together to God and said ... 'And now, Lord, consider their threats, and grant that your servants may speak your word with all boldness, while you stretch out your hand for healing, and signs and wonders are performed through the name of your holy servant Jesus.' When they had prayed, the place where they were assembled was shaken, and they were all filled with the Holy Spirit and began to speak the word of God boldly." (Acts 4:23 - 31)

Most certainly these threatened brothers and sisters in Christ have a way of praying boldly spoken words. The intensity of their earnest prayer is amplified by their unity in the faith.

We tap into the power of God's kingdom when we intentionally join our hearts in prayer to the Father! If we are together, let's pray together!

Family Interaction

Dearly loved children of the Father are brothers and sisters in Christ. We imitate God by walking with each other in sacrificial love. Unified Prayer is one way of loving each other. "Therefore, be imitators of God, as dearly loved children, and walk in love, as Christ also loved us and gave himself for us, a sacrificial and fragrant offering to God." (Ephesians 5:1 - 2)

Think of sitting at the family dinner table, lingering after the meal to engage in lively discussion about current events. The youngest son, Sam, is listening with interest, waiting to interject one particular thought into the conversation. Melody, the middle child, has fresh insight to offer, and Steve waits for just the right moment to deliver his main point of fatherly wisdom. When there is a lull in the conversation, the oldest son, Daniel, puts in his two-cents worth. As typical for a mom, Karen tries to pull it all together with a clear statement of truth. The conversation finally tapers off after everyone has had their say. Each family member leaves the table understanding each other better. All at the table are mutually encouraged by the supportive interaction. Isn't this how we would like all our family conversations to go?

In the family of Christ, this is the reality as we each walk in the love of Christ. Unified Prayer is love-filled family interaction, with our Father at the head of the table, Jesus at our side, and the Holy Spirit joining in to gently direct the conversation. The family members at the table are brothers and sisters in Christ.

GATHER WITH THOSE
IN OUR FAMILY OF BELIEVERS
TO CONVERSE WITH GOD
AND EACH OTHER

"Therefore, you should pray like this: Our Father in heaven, your name be honored as holy." (Matthew 6:9) Not "My Father," nor "Your Father," but "Our Father." Jesus describes the family setting to His disciples when He gives this example of prayer. "Our Father" is the start of Unified Prayer, bringing us to God as a family unit. "Nothing would be more unnatural than that the children of a family should always meet their father separately, but never in the united expression of their desires or their love," according to Andrew Murray.[12]

"These all with one mind were continually devoting themselves to prayer, along with the women, and Mary the mother of Jesus, and with His brothers." (Acts 1:14 NASB) All are praying. They continue in prayer, saturating the soil. They pray with one mind, pursuing agreement in prayer. One speaks and the others agree; another person speaks, and the rest are nodding their heads in mutual understanding. This pattern continues, giving way to each individual voice in the group. Men, women, friends, and family members all unite. They pray together. We are engaged in conversation with each other. The Lord is in our midst. Offer a word of praise, thanksgiving, or repentance. Speak a request, a heart's cry, or a deep concern.

A good conversation has one focus at a time. Water the soil for that one thing and stay with it until the subject has been saturated. We want our prayers to go deep enough to reach the roots. A mere dampening the surface with a passing thought touches the surface only. We can give more. When one subject has been saturated, listen for the Holy Spirit to direct the conversation so that it flows to the next subject matter. This family conversation moves naturally from one point of focus to another.

What if I have more than one thing on my heart to pray about in the group? Pray one thing. Let your brothers and sisters in Christ come alongside you to pray for that one thing, too. When there is a pause, introduce another matter for prayer. By introducing only one subject at a time we can effectively move through this prayer conversation. The result is that every request is saturated in heartfelt prayer, which is an encouragement to all.

We are being built together for God's dwelling in the Spirit. God dwells where we are united together in prayer. "But now in Christ Jesus, you who were far away have been brought near by the blood of Christ. For he is our peace, who made both groups one and tore down the dividing wall of hostility. In his flesh, he made of no effect the law consisting of commands and expressed in regulations, so that he might create in himself one new man from the two, resulting in peace. He did this so that he might reconcile both to God in one body through the cross by which he put the hostility to death. He came and proclaimed the good news of peace to you who were far away and peace to those who were near. For through him we both have access in one Spirit to the Father. So, then, you are no longer foreigners and strangers, but fellow citizens with the saints, and members of God's household, built on the foundation of the apostles and prophets, with Christ Jesus himself as the cornerstone. In him the whole building, being put together, grows into a holy temple in the Lord. In him you are also being built together for God's dwelling in the Spirit." (Ephesians 2:13 - 22)

Ready to Listen

Our prayer together is an active interweaving of spoken words and pauses. It is in this setting that we hear the joys and tears of each other's hearts. Speaking is interspersed with intentional listening.

"After three days, they found him in the temple sitting among the teachers, listening to them and asking them questions." (Luke 2:46) Listening is as important as speaking when we are having a prayer conversation with each other. We see that Jesus is an attentive listener, even at a young age. He is listening and respectfully going deeper in conversation with His questions.

"My dear brothers and sisters, understand this: Everyone should be quick to listen, slow to speak, and slow to anger." (James 1:19) True listening begins when we see others as more important than ourselves. When we operate in the humility of Christ Jesus, we become acutely aware of the needs of others as we pray with them. We are listening to their prayer and listening to the Holy Spirit to know how to pray according to the will of God.

> Do nothing from selfishness or empty conceit, but with humility of mind regard one another as more important than yourselves; do not merely look out for your own personal interests, but also for the interests of others. Have this attitude in yourselves which was also in Christ Jesus, who, although He existed in the form of God, did not regard equality with God a thing to be grasped, but emptied Himself, taking the form of a bond-servant, and being made in the likeness of men. Being found in appearance as a man, He humbled Himself (Philippians 2:3 - 11 NASB).

By listening to one another we honor each other as servants of Christ Jesus. "Whoever listens to you listens to me [Jesus]. Whoever rejects you rejects me. And whoever rejects me rejects the one who sent me." (Luke 10:16)

Quiet words spoken in prayer can have the impact of thunder to our souls. Convicting words from the Holy Spirit are often heard during moments of quiet. Eliminate anything that hinders listening. Come into prayer ready to listen, as disciples who sit at the feet of Jesus. "Mary, who also sat at the Lord's feet and was listening to what he said." (Luke 10:39)

> The words of the wise are heard in quiet, more than the shouting of a ruler is heard among fools. (Ecclesiastes 9:17 NET)

Being of one heart and mind involves being acutely aware of each other and paying close attention to what each one is communicating in prayer. The Holy Spirit brings an awareness that we are all connected to each other in the family of Christ.

"Listen closely, pay attention to the words of the wise, and apply your mind to my knowledge. For it is pleasing if you keep them within you and if they are constantly on your lips." (Proverbs 22:17 - 18) Lean in to hear what the wise have to say. We can learn to pray by listening to the wisdom of others as they pray.

> When they had prayed, the place where they were assembled was shaken, and they were all filled with the Holy Spirit and began to speak the word of God boldly. Now the entire group of those who believed were of one heart and mind, and no one claimed that any of his possessions was his own, but instead they held everything in common. With great power the apostles were giving testimony to the resurrection of the Lord Jesus, and great grace was on all of them. (Acts 4:31 - 33)

Silence

We do not need to have constant talking in our times of Unified Prayer. Allow pauses of silence to be part of the prayer conversation. Waiting quietly is an indicator of trust. Yes, pour out your heart to God in prayer. Turn to Him for refuge. Express your trust in Him at all times, and then quietly pay attention as an expression of faith. "Moses and the Levitical priests spoke to all Israel, 'Be silent, Israel, and listen! This day you have become the people of the Lord your God.'" (Deuteronomy 27:9) It takes a strong man to be quiet. Likewise, it is not easy for a woman to be silent. S. D. Gordan writes, "How few men are strong enough to be able to endure silence. For in silence God is speaking to the inner ear."[13]

Silence helps us listen. Unified Prayer that is punctuated with moments of silence, even awkward silence, help us listen together. Listen to each other and to the Holy Spirit. Being quiet also reminds us not to hurry. Pause. Pauses in discourse help us think. As we pray together, silence gives us moments to reflect on what has been spoken. A pause like this also serves as a natural turning point for someone to introduce a new subject into the prayer conversation. "Patiently wait for God alone, my soul! For he is the one who gives me hope." (Psalm 62:5 NET) "In the morning, Lord, you hear my voice; in the morning I plead my case to you and watch expectantly." (Psalm 5:3)

Short and Simple

We come to Unified Prayer dressed in Christ-like love, which is displayed as mercy, kindness, humility, gentleness, and patience, bearing each other's burdens in prayer. We must remain mindful that we are not praying alone, but in communion with each other. "Therefore, as God's chosen ones, holy and dearly loved, put on compassion, kindness, humility, gentleness, and patience, bearing with one another and forgiving one another" (Colossians 3:12 - 13).

Let the Holy Spirit guide the prayer. He helps us pray together with singular focus, moving in sync with each other in the conversation. We pray together as listeners. Listeners have an awareness of when to stop talking. Unified Prayer is a collection of short sentiments of prayer from the variety of people who are gathered together in the name of the Lord.

This is not the beginning of each family member's conversation with the Lord. It is a continuation of prayers that were begun in private. This means we pray in a way that brings others into the conversation. If we keep our part short and simple, we make room for others to participate. Do you agree with D. L. Moody: "My experience is that those who pray most in their closets generally make short prayers in public."?[14]

We share the meal at our Father's table in the House of Prayer. Let the simple prayers of individual believers form one voice that saturates the soil of every petition.

PRAY EFFECTIVE PRAYERS

Holy Spirit

WHEN OUR PRAYERS ALIGN with God's will we know He hears us. Ask God to reveal His will to you in His word and through the counsel of the Holy Spirit. "This is the confidence we have before him: If we ask anything according to his will, he hears us. And if we know that he hears whatever we ask, we know that we have what we have asked of him." (1 John 5:14 - 15)

Make it your desperate prayer for God to fill you with the Holy Spirit, not for your own benefit, but for those around you who need the Lord. Be persistent. We need the Holy Spirit to direct our prayers. Our friends need us to be filled with the Holy Spirit in order to pray for them most effectively.

"He also said to them, 'Suppose one of you has a friend and goes to him at midnight and says to him, "Friend, lend me three loaves of bread, because a friend of mine on a journey has come to me, and I don't have anything to offer him." Then he will answer from inside and say, "Don't bother me! The door is already locked..." I tell you, even though he won't get up and give him anything because he is his friend, yet because of his friend's shameless boldness, he will get up and give him as much as he needs.'

'So I say to you, ask, and it will be given to you. Seek, and you will find. Knock, and the door will be opened to you. For everyone who asks receives, and the one who seeks finds, and to the one who knocks, the door will be opened. What father among you, if his son asks for a fish, will give him a snake instead of a fish? Or if he asks for an egg, will give him a scorpion? If you then, who are evil, know how to give good gifts to your children, how much more will the heavenly Father give the Holy Spirit to those who ask him?'" (Luke 11:5 - 13) Do we embrace this degree of urgency for our friends who come to us in need of spiritual food? Ask, seek, and knock for the Lord to fill us with the Holy Spirit, to enable us to bring the Bread of Life and the Living Water, Jesus Christ, to our friends and family.

The Holy Spirit gives us guidance as we pray together. We are instructed by the Spirit of Truth, and we follow Him together. "When the Spirit of truth comes, he will guide you into all the truth. For he will not speak on his own, but he will speak whatever he hears. He will also declare to you what is to come. He will glorify me [Jesus], because he will take from what is mine and declare it to you. Everything the Father has is mine. This is why I told you that he takes from what is mine and will declare it to you." (John 16:13 - 15) "My sheep hear my voice, I know them, and they follow me." (John 10:27)

We have examples in the book of Acts where the Holy Spirit gives specific direction to believers who pray together. "As they were worshiping the Lord and fasting, the Holy Spirit said, 'Set apart for me Barnabas and Saul for the work to which I have called them.' Then after they had fasted, prayed, and laid hands on them, they sent them off. So being sent out by the Holy Spirit, they went down to Seleucia, and from there they sailed to Cyprus." (Acts 13:1 - 4)

We join with each other in prayer to seek guidance through the Holy Spirit. For those whose desire is to seek the Lord and obey His instructions, this is a fruitful way to support one another.

Like a Child

Humility is necessary for Unified Prayer, so that we neither dominate the conversation, nor draw back in self-focused timidity. We come united in child-like faith to join the kingdom-minded conversation. "He [Jesus] called a small child and had him stand among them. 'Truly I tell you,' he said, 'unless you turn and become like little children, you will never enter the kingdom of heaven. Therefore, whoever humbles himself like this child—this one is the greatest in the kingdom of heaven.'" (Matthew 18:2 - 4)

We honor each other when we include every willing voice in the conversation. Prayers are measured by faith, not eloquence, so we invite simple prayers. Childlike faith in simple words reaches God's throne and knits believers' hearts together.

PRAYERS ARE MEASURED BY FAITH, NOT ELOQUENCE

Think of the simplicity of some of Jesus' prayers:

"Our Father in heaven, your name be honored as holy." (Matthew 6:9)

"Simon, Simon ... But I have prayed for you that your faith may not fail" (Luke 22:31 - 32).

"He fell facedown and prayed, 'My Father, if it is possible, let this cup pass from me. Yet not as I will, but as you will.'" (Matthew 26:39)

Few words are needed. We are not praying to be noticed by people, so resist the temptation to compare your sentences with someone else's.

Some in our family conversation need to practice saying less, to allow the Holy Spirit to complete the thought through another believer. Others in the conversation need to practice speaking up more, so the Holy Spirit can use their voice to accomplish kingdom purposes. We are all in this together.

This is the how we sit around the table in the House of Prayer.

Group Review and Unified Prayer Guide

Chapter 5: Family

INSTRUCTIONS:

- Read through the chapter review together.
- Please reserve ample time at the end of your gathering for unhurried Unified Prayer (15-30 minutes suggested).

Chapter Review

Prayer is a conversation.

Unified Prayer is one way to love each other as brothers and sisters in Christ. A family sits around the table to have a good conversation. Similarly, we gather with those in our family of believers to converse with God and each other in a prayer conversation.

"Our Father" is the start of Unified Prayer, bringing us to God as a family unit. A good conversation has one focus at a time. Likewise, a prayer conversation moves naturally from one point of focus to another. We come alongside each other to petition the Lord about a certain subject. When there is a pause, someone introduces another subject for prayer. We move through the prayer conversation in this way, introducing one subject after another.

Unified Prayer is a combination of speaking and listening. We are listening to each other's prayer, while also listening to the Holy Spirit so we can pray according to God's will.

Unified Prayer that is punctuated with moments of silence, even awkward silence, help us listen together.

Mindful that we are in a conversation with others, we pray short sentences instead of long paragraphs. If we each keep our part short and simple, we make room for others to participate.

Pray effective prayers.

We need the Holy Spirit to direct our prayers in order to align with God's will. With child-like faith we enter together into the kingdom-minded conversation.

Since prayers are measured by faith, not eloquence, we invite simple prayers. Some of us need to practice saying less. Others in the conversation need to practice speaking up more. Together, the Holy Spirit uses our voices in prayer to accomplish kingdom purposes.

Let's Talk About It

INSTRUCTIONS:

- Read each Scripture.
- Use the accompanying question to discuss how the Scripture relates to prayer.

"After they [Peter and John] were released, they went to their own people and reported everything the chief priests and the elders had said to them. When they heard this, they raised their voices together to God and said, '... And now, Lord, consider their threats, and grant that your servants may speak your word with all boldness, while you stretch out your hand for healing, and signs and wonders are performed through the name of your holy servant Jesus.' When they had prayed, the place where they were assembled was shaken, and they were all filled with the Holy Spirit and began to speak the word of God boldly." (Acts 4:23 - 31)

"When they heard this, they raised their voices ..." Who are *they*? Are they an elite prayer team or are they an assembly of ordinary believers? Notice that these believers raised their voices together to God. Consider these verses as a composite of their prayers, and give an example of how the prayer conversation might flow.

"When the Spirit of truth comes, he will guide you into all the truth. For he will not speak on his own, but he will speak whatever he hears. He will also declare to you what is to come. He will glorify me [Jesus], because he will take from what is mine and declare it to you. Everything the Father has is mine. This is why I told you that he takes from what is mine and will declare it to you." (John 16:13 - 15)

What does the Holy Spirit bring into our prayers?

"He [Jesus] called a small child and had him stand among them. 'Truly I tell you,' he said, 'unless you turn and become like little children, you will never enter the kingdom of heaven. Therefore, whoever humbles himself like this child—this one is the greatest in the kingdom of heaven.'" (Matthew 18:2 - 4)

What are some marks of a child-like prayer?

Let's Talk About It More (as time allows)

"Therefore, you should pray like this: Our Father in heaven, your name be honored as holy." (Matthew 6:9)

What does Jesus' example prayer tell us about the relationship He wants us to have with each other when we pray?

Patiently wait for God alone, my soul! For he is the one who gives me hope. (Psalm 62:5 NET)

How do pauses in a prayer conversation help us patiently wait for God alone?

"Do nothing from selfishness or empty conceit, but with humility of mind regard one another as more important than yourselves; do not merely look out for your own personal interests, but also for the interests of others. Have this attitude in yourselves which was also in Christ Jesus, who, although He existed in the form of God, did not regard equality with God a thing to be grasped, but emptied Himself, taking the form of a bond-servant, and being made in the likeness of men. Being found in appearance as a man, He humbled Himself" (Philippians 2:3 - 8 NASB).

How is listening an act of humility?

"Therefore, as God's chosen ones, holy and dearly loved, put on compassion, kindness, humility, gentleness, and patience, bearing with one another and forgiving one another" (Colossians 3:12 - 13).

In Unified Prayer we are not praying alone, but in communion with others. Explain how compassion, kindness, humility, gentleness, or patience helps you consider how to include others in your prayer conversation.

Unified Prayer Building Blocks

Together:
Pray short simple prayers from the heart. Include all who want to participate.

Family:
This is a prayer conversation. Take turns. Pray one subject at a time. Listen attentively.

Unity:
Support each other with your prayers. Expound on each prayer as the Holy Spirit leads.

Let's Pray Now!

5 Family

Unified Prayer Guide:

INSTRUCTIONS:

- Talk through this guide together.
- Pray, implementing what you have learned.

First Step.

Each person thinks of one or two concerns that have their attention. For example, a difficult conversation you need to have with someone, current world events that are on your mind, or a deadline you face on a project. Consider how to connect the concern you have to the advancement of God's kingdom.

If it helps you, write down a brief note with your thoughts.

Next Step.

Begin by taking turns praying statements of praise to the Lord.

One person steps out by praying a petition in such a way that connects his or her concerns to God's kingdom objectives. Others in the group engage in the prayer conversation.

When there is a pause, another person steps out to pray a petition, and people in the group engage in the prayer conversation on this subject matter. Continue the prayer conversation for as long as time allows.

Concluding Step.

When you sense that everyone has had their say in the prayer conversation, take a moment to be still in the presence of the Lord.

Anyone in the group may offer a simple concluding sentence to the prayer, such as, "We offer our lives for your service, Lord. In Jesus' name we pray, Amen."

We Are in This Together

6. Unity

One heart and mind. *We are in this together.*

WALK IN LOVE

Agree

JESUS PRAYS TO HIS FATHER in the hearing of His twelve disciples. We see the Father answering Jesus' prayer every time we are drawn to walk in loving harmony with each another. His love unites us. "I pray not only for these, but also for those who believe in me through their word. May they all be one, as you, Father, are in me and I am in you... I have given them the glory you have given me, so that they may be one as we are one. I am in them and you are in me, so that they may be made completely one, that the world may know you have sent me and have loved them as you have loved me." (John 17:20 - 23)

In the House of Prayer we "agree to agree" because we are united in essentials of the gospel. Although we may "agree to disagree" over nonessential ideas, Unified Prayer is a safe haven of agreement. We are unified in our desire to seek God's kingdom and His righteousness.

Jesus requires His believers to be in unity with each other. The world sees Jesus when we are completely one with each other, in Him. God's Spirit in us unites us. We are called to do what it takes to keep this unity of the Spirit. "Therefore I [Paul] ... urge you to walk worthy of the calling you have received, with all humility and gentleness, with patience, bearing with one another in love, making every effort to keep the unity of the Spirit through the bond of peace. There is one body and one Spirit—just as you were called to one hope at your calling—one Lord, one faith, one baptism, one God and Father of all, who is above all and through all and in all." (Ephesians 4:1 - 6)

Come to the Lord together in prayer. In the setting of prayer conversation we experience true peace with fellow believers. Unity of the Spirit flourishes when we agree with each other in the presence of God.

All believers must awaken to the urgency of united prayer. We must understand the necessity of this unity to stay faithful to the Lord despite the acceleration of sinful practices in our world. Believers must preserve the unity of the Holy Spirit through one mind in prayer. The Lord's kingdom comes on the prayers of His saints.

"Finally, brothers, rejoice. Aim for restoration, comfort one another, agree with one another, live in peace; and the God of love and peace will be with you." (2 Corinthians 13:11 ESV) There is no better setting than Unified Prayer to rejoice, set things right, and be encouraged as we agree with one another.

One Voice

The concept of one voice is the core principle of Unified Prayer. Exalt His name together. We are united in heart and mind. Separate people who pray separate prayers gain strength as individuals. United people who pray as one voice gain strength as a fellowship of believers. If we are together, let's pray together, and not as mere individuals! Let's put our voices together. "I will bless the Lord at all times; His praise shall continually be in my mouth. My soul will make its boast in the Lord; The humble will hear it and rejoice. O magnify the Lord with me, And let us exalt His name together." (Psalm 34:1 - 3 NASB) When we magnify the Lord together, surely, He hears us. The writings of R. A. Torrey have much to say about prayer, and especially about united prayer. "The prayer that God particularly delights to answer is united prayer. There is power in the prayer of a single individual, and the prayer of individuals has wrought great things, but there is a far greater power in united prayer."[15]

"Now the entire group of those who believed were of one heart and mind" (Acts 4:32). Unity thrives where people gain common ground in prayer. We get to know each other better as we hear prayers from the heart. The vulnerability of honest prayer produces fertile ground for the Father's love to bind us together.

"Therefore, let us approach the throne of grace with boldness, so that we may receive mercy and find grace to help us in time of need." (Hebrews 4:16) Offer praise and thanksgiving, cry with honest repentance, and bring petitions to the Lord. We step arm-in-arm into the throne room together and support each other there as we unite our hearts into one voice.

"Now may the God who gives endurance and encouragement grant you to live in harmony with one another, according to Christ Jesus, so that you may glorify the God and Father of our Lord Jesus Christ with one mind and one voice." (Romans 15:5 - 6) We have a variety of voices joining together with heartfelt expressions of prayer to God. God hears us as one voice giving Him glory. We have unity with one another, and our voices are unanimous in glorifying God. We pray together standing firm in one spirit, with one mind, for advancement of the gospel of Christ.

> Only conduct yourselves in a manner worthy of the gospel of Christ, so that ... I will hear of you that you are standing firm in one spirit, with one mind striving together for the faith of the gospel. (Philippians 1:27 NASB)

When we pray in harmony with each other the Lord hears us as one voice. We see an example of this when musicians join in praise and thanks to the Lord at the completion of the construction of Solomon's temple.

"The trumpeters and singers joined together to praise and thank the Lord with one voice. They raised their voices, accompanied by trumpets, cymbals, and musical instruments, in praise to the Lord: For he is good; his faithful love endures forever. The temple, the Lord temple, was filled with a cloud. And because of the cloud, the priests were not able to continue ministering, for the glory of the Lord filled God's temple." (2 Chronicles 5:13 - 14) They join together with one voice. There are many voices singing loudly and various musical instruments. This musical masterpiece is heard as one voice giving praise to God.

> After they were released, they went to their own people and reported everything the chief priests and the elders had said to them. When they heard this, they raised their voices together to God and said, "Master, you are the one who made the heaven, the earth, and the sea, and everything in them... And now, Lord, consider their threats, and grant that your servants may speak your word with all boldness, while you stretch out your hand for healing, and signs and wonders are performed through the name of your holy servant Jesus." When they had prayed, the place where they were assembled was shaken, and they were all filled with the Holy Spirit and began to speak the word of God boldly. (Acts 4:23 - 31)

This close-knit family of believers raises their voices together to God. This is their first response to the pressing threat of persecution. Remember, also, that these believers are seeing massive numbers of people coming to faith through the preaching of the gospel. In this room multiple voices are united as one. Notice their prayer. It may be happening like this: One person starts with words of praise, "Master, we worship you as Creator of heaven and earth." Others join in with similar phrases. "You made the heaven, the earth, the sea and everything in them." Someone begins offering a request, "Lord, grant us boldness despite the threats." Someone else agrees, "We need boldness to speak your word." And, "Lord, make yourself known by healing the sick." "Perform signs and wonders, Lord, so even more people will believe the gospel message we are proclaiming."

Notice God's response to their united voices in prayer. There is a fresh filling of the Holy Spirit, and the people are granted boldness to speak the word of God. The Lord makes His presence known to all in the room.

Unhindered

Remember that we are praying together for kingdom purposes. Pray for our government and for those in authority, so that we may preach the gospel unhindered. God wants all men to be saved and to hear the truth of the gospel. "First of all, then, I urge that petitions, prayers, intercessions, and thanksgivings be made for everyone, for kings and all those who are in authority, so that we may lead a tranquil and quiet life in all godliness and dignity. This is good, and it pleases God our Savior, who wants everyone to be saved and to come to the knowledge of the truth." (1 Timothy 2:1 - 4)

We must constantly fight for unity by refusing to fight each other. We are united by having the same kingdom mindset and purpose given to us by our Lord Jesus Christ. "I urge you, brothers and sisters, by the name of our Lord Jesus Christ, to agree together, to end your divisions, and to be united by the same mind and purpose." (1 Corinthians 1:10 NET)

Be aware that resentments, disputes, and gossip among us hinder our prayers. Petty differences always seem relevant. Know that the enemy uses these disturbances to divert our attention away from our crucial kingdom-minded focus. Unified Prayer is based on agreement. Political, religious, and cultural quarrels break the Christ-pleasing bond of unity in prayer. Our prayers reach higher than these earthly perspectives. We adopt a heavenly-kingdom view to pray for God's will to come to pass. Remember that the salvation of people's souls is at stake. For this reason, we must firmly resist all efforts, fleshly and otherwise, to derail our divine purpose for Unified Prayer. "Have nothing to do with foolish, ignorant controversies; you know that they breed quarrels." (2 Timothy 2:23 ESV) "Therefore, I want the men in every place to pray, lifting up holy hands without anger or argument." (1 Timothy 2:8) "Examine me, O Lord, and test me. Evaluate my inner thoughts and motives." (Psalm 26:2 NET)

RESIST ALL EFFORTS TO DERAIL
OUR DIVINE PURPOSE FOR UNIFIED PRAYER

Here in the House of Prayer we are all on the same side. We are in Christ, and Christ is in us. "In Christ there is not Greek and Jew, circumcision and uncircumcision, barbarian, Scythian, slave and free; but Christ is all and in all. Therefore, as God's chosen ones, holy and dearly loved, put on compassion, kindness, humility, gentleness, and patience, bearing with one another and forgiving one another if anyone has a grievance against another. Just as the Lord has forgiven you, so you are also to forgive. Above all, put on love, which is the perfect bond of unity. And let the peace of Christ, to which you were also called in one body, rule your hearts. And be thankful." (Colossians 3:11 - 15)

Side by Side

We are better together. With our hearts knit tightly together, we feel each other's pain. When one of us unravels, it affects all of us. When someone among us experiences a victory, the rest of us are running along in the victory lap. Prayer aligns our hearts with each other in these life experiences. "So if one member suffers, all the members suffer with it; if one member is honored, all the members rejoice with it." (1 Corinthians 12:26)

In our community of believers, no one should be alone. In Unified Prayer, when a brother or sister in Christ is suffering, the rest of us enter into that suffering with them by saturating their deep need in prayer. When one of us is celebrating, everyone participates in the prayer to express a thankful heart along with our believing friend.

"And we exhort you, brothers and sisters: warn those who are idle, comfort the discouraged, help the weak, be patient with everyone ... always pursue what is good for one another and for all. Rejoice always, pray constantly, give thanks in everything; for this is God's will for you in Christ Jesus. Don't stifle the Spirit" (1 Thessalonians 5:14 - 22). Think of these essential instructions for Christ's body as starting points for Unified Prayer. We walk side by side through life's circumstances, praying each other through. Warning, comforting, helping, being patient, pursuing what is good for each other, rejoicing, giving thanks, welcoming the Spirit. Inserted in the list is "pray constantly." Do you see how the healthy rhythm of Unified Prayer in the body of Christ keeps us aligned with God's kingdom objectives?

Come together with a posture of praise. We serve the Lord side by side. Even in dark times we lift our hands to the Lord to give Him praise. Praising the Lord together strengthens our bond with each other.

> Now bless the Lord, all you servants of the Lord who stand in the Lord's house at night! Lift up your hands in the holy place and bless the Lord! May the Lord, Maker of heaven and earth, bless you from Zion. (Psalm 134:1 - 3)

WE ARE ONE IN THE SPIRIT

Harvest

WE CAN ALWAYS AGREE on the things God's word tells us to pray about. One thing Jesus tells us to pray about is the Lord's harvest of souls.

"Then he [Jesus] said to his disciples, 'The harvest is abundant, but the workers are few. Therefore, pray to the Lord of the harvest to send out workers into his harvest.'" (Matthew 9:37 - 38) Pray for more workers for the Lord's harvest fields. Pray for confidence to boldly proclaim the gospel. Pray for the knowledge of God's will, and spiritual wisdom and understanding, and that believers would bear good fruit and be strengthened with power for God's glory. There is no shortage of things we can agree on in prayer.

> Jesus said to them, "My food is to do the will of the one who sent me and to complete his work. Don't you say, 'There are four more months and then comes the harvest?' I tell you, look up and see that the fields are already white for harvest!" (John 4:34 - 35 NET)

> Pray also for me, that the message may be given to me when I open my mouth to make known with boldness the mystery of the gospel. For this I am an ambassador in chains. Pray that I might be bold enough to speak about it as I should. (Ephesians 6:19 - 20)

> For this reason also, since the day we heard this, we haven't stopped praying for you. We are asking that you may be filled with the knowledge of his will in all wisdom and spiritual understanding, so that

> you may walk worthy of the Lord, fully pleasing to him: bearing fruit in every good work and growing in the knowledge of God, being strengthened with all power, according to his glorious might, so that you may have great endurance and patience, joyfully giving thanks to the Father, who has enabled you to share in the saints' inheritance in the light. (Colossians 1:9 - 12)

Jesus Is Here

"Who has a prayer request?" After every person with a need speaks up, we assign different people to pray for each of the different requests, or we write it all down, or we open the floor for prayer and try to remember every request. We can improve on this.

"Again, truly I tell you, if two of you on earth agree about any matter that you pray for, it will be done for you by my Father in heaven. For where two or three are gathered together in my name, I am there among them." (Matthew 18:19 - 20) Let us shift our approach to one that has less talking to each other about the requests and more conversation with the Lord in Unified Prayer. It's this simple: We make a setting where every believer is encouraged to pray what is on their heart. Instead of saying my prayer request to the people in the group, I pray my petition to the Lord, with the people listening. When a believer prays to the Lord in his own words it deepens his relationship with God. Isn't that what we want to encourage in our faith family? The Father already knows the need. The rest of us are there to add supporting prayers. We can do that by hearing a simple prayer from the heart.

"Jesus stopped, called them, and said, 'What do you want me to do for you?'" (Matthew 20:32) (See also Mark 10:36; Mark 10:51; Luke 18:41) Let this question guide the person who has a need to introduce in prayer: What do you want Jesus to do for you? Make it a practice to help each other take every need directly to the Lord. Each person speaks to the Lord in simple words, and we all join the conversation with prayers of faith. To saturate in prayer means we talk to the Lord about each particular need, letting different perspectives join the conversation. We continue in focused attention as we rely on the Holy Spirit to direct us to fully cover the subject, one subject at a time.

What if no one can think of anything to pray about? The room is quiet, and no one breaks the silence. Remember our assignment from the Lord to ask to for more workers for the Lord's harvest fields. At the very least, this is common ground for believers to raise a petition to the Lord. Another way to prompt participation is to ask, "What have you been praying about on your own?" When we let our brothers and sisters join in on those prayers that were begun in private, we are inviting the Lord to knit our hearts together in His name.

Jesus is here, right here among us when we pray. Can you see His head nodding in agreement with us?

Our Father Knows

Remember that our Father knows our needs. When we gather around a brother or sister in Christ to saturate their need in prayer, we are asking for the Father's will to be done in their life. "Behold, how good and how pleasant it is for brothers to dwell together in unity! It is like the precious oil upon the head, coming down upon the beard, even Aaron's beard, coming down upon the edge of his robes. It is like the dew of Hermon coming down upon the mountains of Zion; For there the Lord commanded the blessing—life forever." (Psalm 133:1 - 3 NASB)

We hear the need, and we hear what the Holy Spirit is saying through another believer's prayer. We support one another by developing the thought of each prayed request. We can learn to do this effectively with these simple **Y.E.S.** strategies:

"Lord, please heal my mother who is very ill."

Y. *Your own words.* Simply repeat the prayer in your own words. "Lord, you have the power to heal. Please bring healing to my friend's mother."

E. *Express agreement.* Verbally agree with what is said. "Lord, I agree with my friend's prayer that You heal her mother."

S. *Specific Focus.* Unwrap what you hear about the need and ask the Holy Spirit to reveal specifics for focused prayer. "Lord, let your peace rule and reign in the life of my friend's mother. Please lift her worries."

WE CONTINUE
IN FOCUSED ATTENTION
AS WE RELY ON THE HOLY SPIRIT
TO DIRECT US

"I post watchmen on your walls, O Jerusalem; they should keep praying all day and all night. You who pray to the Lord, don't be silent!" (Isaiah 62:6 NET) Relentless prayer is when someone is praying day and night out of desperation. We can have that intensity when we focus on a particular need in Unified Prayer. There is no need to work up emotion. We also need not suppress true emotion as we pray, for tears can be an indicator of the Holy Spirit's work below the surface in our hearts. Let us allow the Lord to bring a calming peace among us as we pray together, assuring us of His attentive ear.

"Now he told them a parable on the need for them to pray always and not give up ... Will not God grant justice to his elect who cry out to him day and night? Will he delay helping them?" (Luke 18:1, 7) Continue in prayer together with one mind. Where the water saturates the soil the plants flourish. Roots grow. Plants bear fruit and reproduce. We are saturated with the blessings of unity when we pray in agreement with each other.

> Then they returned to Jerusalem from the Mount of Olives, which is near Jerusalem—a Sabbath day's journey away. When they arrived, they went to the room upstairs where they were staying: Peter, John, James, Andrew, Philip, Thomas, Bartholomew, Matthew, James the son of Alphaeus, Simon the Zealot, and Judas the son of James. They all were

continually united in prayer, along with the women, including Mary the mother of Jesus, and his brothers. (Acts 1:12 - 14)

This is how we are united in the Father's House of Prayer.

Group Review and Unified Prayer Guide

Chapter 6: Unity

INSTRUCTIONS:

- Read through the chapter review together.
- Please reserve ample time at the end of your gathering for unhurried Unified Prayer (15-30 minutes suggested).

Chapter Review

Walk in love.

The love of Jesus unites us. Unity of the Spirit flourishes when we agree with each other in the presence of God through Unified Prayer.

If we are together, let's pray together, and not as mere individuals.

We must fight for unity by refusing to fight each other. We are united by having the same kingdom mindset and purpose given to us by our Lord Jesus Christ. Unified Prayer is based on agreement. We must resist all efforts, fleshly and otherwise, to derail our divine purpose for unified prayer. We are all on the same side. We are in Christ, and Christ is in us.

We walk side by side through life's circumstances, praying each other through.

We are one in the Spirit.

In Unified Prayer every believer prays directly to the Lord. Instead of listing prayer requests to each other, we pray our petitions to the Lord. We each speak to the Lord in simple words and all join the conversation with prayers of faith. We rely on the Holy Spirit to direct us to cover each subject, one subject at a time. We join each other in prayer and the Lord knits us together.

We can learn to pray together effectively using any of these simple **Y.E.S.** strategies:

"Lord, please heal my mother who is very ill."

Y. *Your own words.* Simply repeat the prayer in your own words. "Lord, you have the power to heal. Please bring healing to my friend's mother."

E. *Express agreement.* Verbally agree with what is said. "Lord, I agree with my friend's prayer that you heal her mother."

S. *Specific focus.* Ask the Holy Spirit to reveal specifics for focused prayer. "Lord, let your peace rule and reign in the life of my friend's mother. Please lift her worries."

We are saturated with the blessings of unity when we pray in agreement with each other.

Let's Talk About It

INSTRUCTIONS:

- Read each Scripture.
- Use the accompanying question to discuss how the Scripture relates to prayer.

"I pray not only for these, but also for those who believe in me through their word. May they all be one, as you, Father, are in me and I am in you... I have given them the glory you have given me, so that they may be one as we are one. I am in them and you are in me, so that they may be made completely one, that the world may know you have sent me and have loved them as you have loved me." (John 17:20 - 23)

Why does Jesus want His followers to be one with each other? How will the world know that God loves us?

"Now may the God who gives endurance and encouragement grant you to live in harmony with one another, according to Christ Jesus, so that you may glorify the God and Father of our Lord Jesus Christ with one mind and one voice." (Romans 15:5 - 6)

How does it glorify God when we come to Him with one mind and one voice? How can people with differing opinions, backgrounds, and personalities pray in harmony with one another?

"Then they returned to Jerusalem from the Mount of Olives, which is near Jerusalem—a Sabbath day's journey away. When they arrived, they went to the room upstairs where they were staying: Peter, John, James, Andrew, Philip, Thomas, Bartholomew, Matthew, James the son of Alphaeus, Simon the Zealot, and Judas the son of James. They all were continually united in prayer, along with the women, including Mary the mother of Jesus, and his brothers." (Acts 1:12 - 14)

"They were all continually united in prayer." What are some of the differences between the various people in this upstairs room? What do all these people have in common?

Let's Talk About It More (as time allows)

"Therefore, let us approach the throne of grace with boldness, so that we may receive mercy and find grace to help us in time of need." (Hebrews 4:16)

What is the benefit of us approaching the throne of grace together?

"So if one member suffers, all the members suffer with it; if one member is honored, all the members rejoice with it." (1 Corinthians 12:26)

How does it help you when you hear other believers joining in prayer for your needs? Why does your participation in Unified Prayer help someone else know they are not alone?

"Then he [Jesus] said to his disciples, 'The harvest is abundant, but the workers are few. Therefore, pray to the Lord of the harvest to send out workers into his harvest.'" (Matthew 9:37 - 38)

Where do you see a harvest field? How would you like to see the Lord answer this prayer for more harvest workers?

"Again, truly I tell you, if two of you on earth agree about any matter that you pray for, it will be done for you by my Father in heaven. For where two or three are gathered together in my name, I am there among them." (Matthew 18:19 - 20)

What does it mean to be gathered together in Jesus' name? Where is Jesus when you voice a prayer, and others agree with your prayer?

Unified Prayer Building Blocks

Together:
Pray short simple prayers from the heart. Include all who want to participate.

Family:
This is a prayer conversation. Take turns. Pray one subject at a time. Listen attentively.

Unity:
Support each other with your prayers. Expound on each prayer as the Holy Spirit leads.

Let's Pray Now!

6 Unity

Unified Prayer Guide:

INSTRUCTIONS:

- Talk through this guide together.
- Pray, implementing what you have learned.

First Step.

Each person thinks about the name of a community, location, or people group wherein they want to see the Lord bring a harvest of souls for Jesus Christ.

If it helps you, write down the name of the "harvest field" you have in mind.

____

Next Step.

Begin by taking turns praying statements of praise to the Lord, especially focusing on God as Lord of the Harvest.

One person steps out by asking the Lord of the Harvest to send laborers into the harvest field that is on his or her heart. Others in the group engage in the prayer conversation.

When there is a pause, someone else step out to pray for another harvest area, and people in the group engage in the prayer conversation. Continue the prayer conversation for as long as time allows.

Concluding Step.

When you sense that everyone has had their say in the prayer conversation, take a moment to be still in the presence of the Lord.

Anyone in the group may offer a simple concluding sentence to the prayer, such as, "Turn our hearts, Lord, to desire Your will in all things. In Jesus' name we pray, Amen."

Power of Prayer

HOUSE OF PRAYER
EST.

7. Established

COME INTO GOD'S PRESENCE

Intimately Acquainted in Alone Prayer

PRAYERS THAT SATURATE THE SOIL, that intentionally linger before God, that ask Him to pour His grace into the need at hand, are prayers that accomplish kingdom purposes. These prayers come from people who know God's ears are attentive to their prayers. These are people who know God intimately because they constantly come into His royal courts. They understand that His call for persistence in prayer is directly related to trusting Him fully.

> For a day in Your courts is better than a thousand outside. I would rather stand at the threshold of the house of my God Than dwell in the tents of wickedness. For the Lord God is a sun and shield; The Lord gives grace and glory; No good thing does He withhold from those who walk uprightly. O Lord of hosts, How blessed is the man who trusts in You! (Psalm 84:10 - 12 NASB)

Keep your relationship with God the most important thing in your life. The reward the Father has for you in this secret place cannot be found in any other pursuit. Dr. Leonard Ravenhill once said, "The secret of praying is praying in secret."[16]

"But when you pray, go into your private room, shut your door, and pray to your Father who is in secret. And your Father who sees in secret will reward you." (Matthew 6:6) Our Father meets us in secret to give us wise counsel and to make His ways known to us. Think of walking with Him out in the garden, conversing with Him and enjoying His presence. I imagine that is what the early days were like for Adam, when he walked in purity with God in that very first garden. God keeps beckoning us to come and walk in personal fellowship with Him.

Let this be our desire, as it was for prayer warrior Andrew Murray: "Oh let the place of secret prayer become to me the most beloved spot on earth."[17]

> I have asked one thing from the Lord; it is what I desire: to dwell in the house of the Lord all the days of my life, gazing on the beauty of the Lord and seeking him in his temple. For he will conceal me in his shelter in the day of adversity; he will hide me under the cover of his tent; he will set me high on a rock. Then my head will be high above my enemies around me; I will offer sacrifices in his tent with shouts of joy. I will sing and make music to the Lord. Lord, hear my voice when I call; be gracious to me and answer me. My heart says this about you: "Seek his face." Lord, I will seek your face. (Psalm 27:4 - 8)

In this sheltered place where we meet the Lord privately, He satisfies our deepest longings, saturating our souls with living water. His teaching falls on us like rain, His word settles on us like dew, and His gentle rain showers on us to bring continued growth for flourishing in His kingdom. "Pay attention, heavens, and I will speak; listen, earth, to the words from my mouth. Let my teaching fall like rain and my word settle like dew, like gentle rain on new grass and showers on tender plants. For I will proclaim the Lord's name. Declare the greatness of our God!" (Deuteronomy 32:1 - 3)

Again, from Andrew Murray: "True prayer that takes hold of God's strength, that availeth much, to which the gates of heaven are really opened wide—who would not cry, 'Oh, for someone to teach me thus to pray?'"[18]

One Heart and Mind in Unified Prayer

Each person in the upper room gathering has a personal connection with Jesus. As friends, disciples, and family members, all have first-hand experience with the grace and truth of the living Jesus Christ. Likewise, our first-hand experience with Jesus gives us a shared foundation for Unified Prayer. "Then they returned to Jerusalem from the mountain called the Mount of Olives (which is near Jerusalem, a Sabbath day's journey away). When they had entered Jerusalem, they went to the upstairs room where they were staying. Peter and John, and James, and Andrew, Philip and Thomas, Bartholomew and Matthew, James son of Alphaeus and Simon the Zealot, and Judas son of James were there. All these continued together in prayer with one mind, together with the women, along with Mary the mother of Jesus, and his brothers." (Acts 1:12 - 14 NET)

Effective Alone Prayer is necessary for effective Unified Prayer. When each believer is personally acquainted with the Lord's presence, we all come to the Lord on common ground. "My heart has heard you say, 'Come and talk with me.' And my heart responds, 'Lord, I am coming.'" (Psalm 27:8 NLT)

When we come together as united brothers and sisters in Christ we step into the reality of God's favor and grace. In this realm we experience the presence of God as His united children through Unified Prayer. We get to enjoy the presence of God together, as "it is the work of the Holy Spirit, when you and I pray, to take us by the hand as it were, and lead us into the very presence of God and introduce us to Him, and to make God real to us as we pray," according to Andrew Murray.[19]

Who do we find praying together in that upstairs room in Jerusalem? All eleven apostles are named. Other men and women are in the room with them. These believers saturate the soil together in prayer as they linger in the Lord's presence with one heart and mind. They are waiting together. Maybe their prayer sounded like thoughts from Psalm 25.

"Make your ways known to me, Lord; teach me your paths. Guide me in your truth and teach me, for you are the God of my salvation; I wait for you all day long." (Psalm 25:4 - 5) Pray in secret to be able to pray together. Personal intimate prayer is the flame that ignites powerful Unified Prayer. Pray in secret when you are alone. Pray together when you are together. Pray together to be able to pray in secret. Powerful Unified Prayer revives personal intimate prayer. Pray alone, pray together. This is the melodic rhythm of faith that enriches the Bride of Christ. This is what dependence on God looks like. This is the Spirit that fills the House of Prayer.

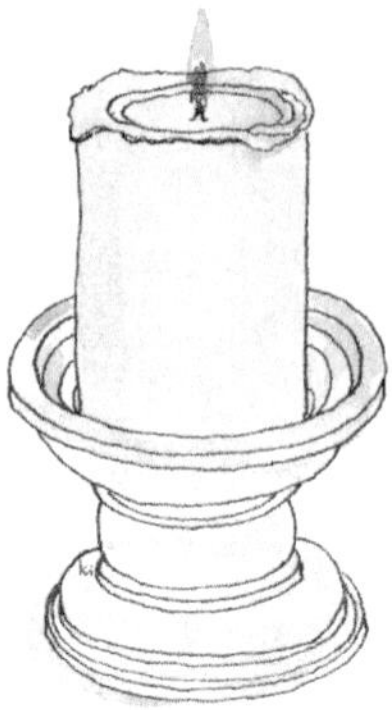

PERSONAL INTIMATE PRAYER
IS THE FLAME THAT IGNITES
POWERFUL UNIFIED PRAYER

When abiding-in-Christ believers join in prayer, there is nothing to hinder the powerful unity through the Holy Spirit for which God has designed us. These saturated souls are knit together for kingdom purposes.

CALL ON GOD'S POWER

Seek the Kingdom of God

JESUS TELLS HIS DISCIPLES that worry is not appropriate for His followers. Pray from faith, not from worry. Do not pursue what the rest of the world pursues. Know that your heavenly Father is committed to caring for all your needs. "Therefore I tell you: Don't worry about your life ... Consider the birds of the sky: They don't sow or reap or gather into barns, yet your heavenly Father feeds them. Aren't you worth more than they? Can any of you add one moment to his life span by worrying? ... So don't worry, saying, 'What will we eat?' or 'What will we drink?' or 'What will we wear?'

For the Gentiles eagerly seek all these things, and your heavenly Father knows that you need them. But seek first the kingdom of God and his righteousness, and all these things will be provided for you. Therefore don't worry about tomorrow, because tomorrow will worry about itself" (Matthew 6:25 - 34).

Go after the things that matter for His kingdom. Pursue righteousness. Pursue souls for His kingdom. Let this attention on heavenly pursuits be the thread that runs through your prayers. Pursue His kingdom first.

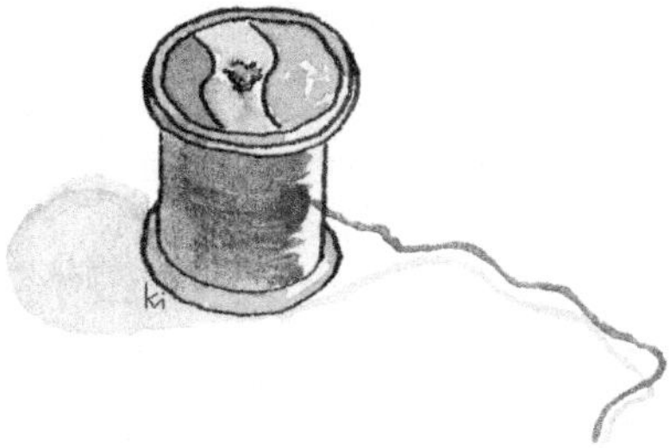

ATTENTION ON HEAVENLY PURSUITS
IS THE THREAD
THAT RUNS THROUGH OUR PRAYERS

After Jesus suffered for our sins, and He returned and appeared to His disciples, what did He speak to them about? What message did Jesus emphasize before leaving them for His Kingly position in heaven? "I wrote ... about all that Jesus began to do and teach until the day he was taken up ... After he had suffered, he also presented himself alive to them by many convincing proofs, appearing to them over a period of forty days and speaking about the kingdom of God." (Acts 1:1 - 3)

He is speaking to us about the kingdom of God. This is what matters to our Lord Jesus.

Pray Together Often

Constant prayer is woven in the fabric of a healthy body of believers. Notice the apostle Paul's requests for prayer. Paul assumes as he writes to the churches that they pray together, and that they will pray for him and for his fellow servants of the Lord Jesus. "Rejoice always, pray constantly, give thanks in everything; for this is God's will for you in Christ Jesus. Don't stifle the Spirit" (1 Thessalonians 5:16 - 19).

We learn by reading the letters of the apostle Paul that Paul expects church families to pray for him. He treats it as an essential part of the community of believers' united activities. Paul is known to be serious about prayer, so much so, that he depends on those who pray for him. He knew the necessity of Unified Prayer on his behalf for the sake of the gospel. E. M. Bounds writes that Paul "asks, he covets, he pleads in an impassioned way for the help of all God's saints. He knew that in the spiritual realm, as elsewhere, in union there is strength; that the concentration and aggregation of faith, desire, and prayer increased the volume of spiritual force until it became overwhelming and irresistible in its power."[20]

To the church family in Rome: "Now I appeal to you, brothers and sisters, through our Lord Jesus Christ and through the love of the Spirit, to strive together with me in prayers to God on my behalf." (Romans 15:30)

To the church family in Corinth: "While you join in helping us by your prayers" (2 Corinthians 1:11).

To the church family in Ephesus: "Pray also for me, that the message may be given to me when I open my mouth to make known with boldness the mystery of the gospel." (Ephesians 6:19)

To the church family in Philippi: "I know that this will turn out for my deliverance through your prayers and the provision of the Spirit of Jesus Christ." (Philippians 1:19 NASB)

To the church family in Colossae: "At the same time, pray also for us that God may open a door to us for the word, to speak the mystery of Christ, for which I am in chains." (Colossians 4:3)

To the church family in Thessalonica: "In addition, brothers and sisters, pray for us that the word of the Lord may spread rapidly and be honored, just as it was with you." (2 Thessalonians 3:1)

Give Unified Prayer First Place

The time to pray is now! The spiritual battle lines are drawn. The faithful are summoned to join the tactical forces of Unified Prayer. Each of us is responsible to initiate this call for prayer among our fellow soldiers of the Lord. "Take the helmet of salvation and the sword of the Spirit—which is the word of God. Pray at all times in the Spirit with every prayer and request, and stay alert with all perseverance and intercession for all the saints." (Ephesians 6:17 - 18)

Through Unified Prayer we petition our King of Kings to saturate the dry ground around us. Through Unified Prayer we gain victory over enemy tactics. Through Unified Prayer we march in sync with each other, unstoppable. According to S. D. Gordon, "We think we can do more where we are through our service: then prayer to give power to service. No—with the blackest underscoring of emphasis, let it be said—no. We can do no thing of real power until we have done the prayer thing."[21]

We must not simply wait for opportunities to pray. We must make opportunities to pray. Initiate Unified Prayer whenever possible. Call some friends to come over to your home for a time of prayer. Volunteer to lead prayer in your small group or Bible study group. Grab a few friends in the hallway before a church service to pray for the pastor, to pray for lost souls, to pray for families. When you hear of a crisis in your church family, gather people in your home to pray. Be the one who turns the tide in your area that awakens believers to pray. Spark a prayer revival!

ENTER IN

House of Prayer

TAKE OFF YOUR SHOES when you enter the house. The House of Prayer is holy ground. Entering Unified Prayer with worship on our lips is leaving our "shoes at the door."

"'Do not come closer,' he said. 'Remove the sandals from your feet, for the place where you are standing is holy ground.'" (Exodus 3:5) We take off our shoes with the world's soil on our souls as we bow low before our King. Offering our sacrifice of praise before we introduce any petition is the appropriate way to approach our King.

> Acknowledge that the Lord is God. He made us, and we are his—his people, the sheep of his pasture. Enter his gates with thanksgiving and his courts with praise. Give thanks to him and bless his name. For the Lord

> is good, and his faithful love endures forever; his faithfulness, through all generations. (Psalm 100:3 - 5)

Praise is saying what we know is true about God. It is that simple. "I praise you, Lord" is often the first words we think to say. We can say much more, then, as we reflect on who God is and the wondrous aspects of His nature.

"Lord, you are God."

"Lord, you made us, and we are yours."

"Lord, you are the Good Shepherd."

"You are King and we offer you thanksgiving and praise."

"We bless your Name. Your Name is above every name."

"Lord, you are good."

"Lord, your faithful love endures forever."

"Lord, you are faithful."

"Lord, your faithfulness endures through all generations."

Leaving self-centered thoughts aside, we raise our voices together as one to give all attention, honor, and praise to the One who is worthy of it all.

> Our Father in heaven, your name be honored as holy. (Matthew 6:9)

We honor our Father in heaven when we begin Unified Prayer with expressions of worship. We see this practice in the prayers of the disciples in the early church. "After they were released, they went to their own people and reported everything ... When they heard this, they raised their voices together to God and said, 'Master, you are the one who made the heaven, the earth, and the sea, and everything in them.'" (Acts 4:23 - 24)

And then, we sit at the table in the Father's house and dine together, having conversation, bringing our faith-filled petitions to our Lord who has invited us to be with Him here.

> The Lord is my shepherd, I lack nothing. He takes me to lush pastures, he leads me to refreshing water. He restores my strength. He leads me down the right paths for the sake of his reputation. Even when I must walk through the darkest valley, I fear no danger, for you are with me; your rod and your staff reassure me. You prepare a feast before me in plain sight of my enemies. You refresh my head with oil; my cup is completely full. Surely your goodness and faithfulness will pursue me

all my days, and I will live in the Lord's house for the rest of my life. (Psalm 23 NET)

Let us dwell in the Father's house.

To construct this House of Prayer remember three simple building blocks. These essentials lay the groundwork for harmonious prayer in a community of believers.

1. **Together:** We are the body of Christ. *Praying out loud joins us together in faith.*

2. **Family:** We are brothers and sisters in Christ. *Conversation in prayer joins us together in love.*

3. **Unity:** We are one in Christ. *Agreement in prayer joins us together in unity.*

Now may the God who gives endurance and encouragement grant you to live in harmony with one another, according to Christ Jesus, so that you may glorify the God and Father of our Lord Jesus Christ with one mind and one voice. (Romans 15:5 - 6)

Jesus Is Here

What does the House of Prayer look like? Open the door to look inside. Where there is a House of Prayer community we see a familiar practice of prayer. We notice a culture of prayer. We hear a lot of asking, seeking, and knocking. These praying disciples think of Unified Prayer as an essential activity in their community. "Ask, and it will be given to you. Seek, and you will find. Knock, and the door will be opened to you. For everyone who asks receives, and the one who seeks finds, and to the one who knocks, the door will be opened. Who among you, if his son asks him for bread, will give him a stone? Or if he asks for a fish, will give him a snake? If you then, who are evil, know how to give good gifts to your children, how much more will your Father in heaven give good things to those who ask him." (Matthew 7:7 - 11)

OPEN THE DOOR
TO THE HOUSE OF PRAYER
AND SEE THAT JESUS IS HERE

Where is the House of Prayer? Church building, home, small group location, coffee shop, office building, neighborhood clubhouse, children's playground, street corner, you name it. The House of Prayer is anywhere believers are together.

We must understand that prayer is not something we add to our work to keep everything going right. Instead, as Andrew Murray writes, we must "pray much and then to work enough for the power and blessing obtained in prayer to find its way through us to men."[22]

"O Lord, I cry out to you. Come quickly to me. Pay attention to me when I cry out to you. May you accept my prayer like incense, my uplifted hands like the evening offering." (Psalm 141:1 - 2 NET) We offer our prayer as incense to God. May the Lord receive our prayer as a pleasing aroma before His throne. May the Lord see our upraised hands as our willingness to honor Him. (See Exodus 30:8; Luke 1:10; Revelation 5:8; Revelation 8:3-4)

What is Jesus' view of the House of Prayer? Even at age twelve, the maturing Jesus understands that His Father's house is the place to sit among teachers, listen, and interact by asking pertinent questions. Jesus has always been about His Father's business. "'Why were you searching for me?' he [Jesus] asked them. 'Didn't you know that it was necessary for me to be in my Father's house?'" (Luke 2:49)

Shortly before offering up His life on the cross Jesus again reminds everyone about His Father's intentions for the Lord's house of worship. "He [Jesus] said to them, 'It is written, my house will be called a house of prayer'" (Matthew 21:13).

Is the House of Prayer a building? No, the House of Prayer is wherever believers are together. "So, then, you are no longer foreigners and strangers, but fellow citizens with the saints, and members of God's household, built on the foundation of the apostles and prophets, with Christ Jesus himself as the cornerstone. In him the whole building, being put together, grows into a holy temple in the Lord. In him you are also being built together for God's dwelling in the Spirit." (Ephesians 2:19 - 22)

> Again, truly I [Jesus] tell you, if two of you on earth agree about any matter that you pray for, it will be done for you by my Father in heaven. For where two or three are gathered together in my name, I am there among them. (Matthew 18:19 - 20)

Do we not know that Jesus is about His Father's business? Always. "Jesus came near and said to them, 'All authority has been given to me in heaven and on earth. Go, therefore, and make disciples of all nations, baptizing them in the name of the Father and of the Son and of the Holy Spirit, teaching them to observe everything I have commanded you. And remember, I am with you always, to the end of the age.'" (Matthew 28:18 - 20) "Didn't you know that I must be in my Father's house?" (Luke 2:49 NET)

Come join us in the House of Prayer. Jesus is here.

Unified Prayer Guide and Group Review

Chapter 7: Established

INSTRUCTIONS:

- Please begin with prayer.
- Allow time at the end of your gathering for the *Chapter Review* and *Let's Talk About It.*
- Talk through the *Unified Prayer Guide* together.
- Pray, implementing what you have learned.

Unified Prayer Building Blocks

Together:
Pray short simple prayers from the heart. Include all who want to participate.

Family:
This is a prayer conversation. Take turns. Pray one subject at a time. Listen attentively.

Unity:
Support each other with your prayers. Expound on each prayer as the Holy Spirit leads.

Let's Pray Now!

Unified Prayer Guide:

First Step.

Spend a few moments in silence, each person thinking about some of the requests they have brought to the Lord in their times of Alone Prayer in the last few days.

Silently ask the Lord to guide the group by His Holy Spirit through a time of prayer that aligns with God's will and His kingdom purposes.

Write down some of your thoughts if that will help you voice your prayer in the group setting.

Next Step.

Begin by taking turns praying statements of praise to the Lord. Give the Lord heartfelt worship, focusing on His glorious splendor and holiness. Do not hurry this step. Enjoy resting in the presence of the Lord as you hear words of praise come from your brothers and sisters in Christ.

One person steps out by presenting a concise request to the Lord. Others in the group enter into the prayer conversation.

When there is a pause, another person presents a request to the Lord, and others in the group engage by contributing to the prayer.

Do not hurry. Enjoy participating in a meaningful prayer conversation.

Concluding Step.

When you sense that everyone has had their say in the prayer conversation, take a moment to be still in the presence of the Lord.

Anyone in the group may offer a simple concluding sentence to the prayer, such as, "Thank you, Lord, for inviting us into your presence to be with You. In Jesus' name we pray, Amen."

7 Established

Chapter Review

INSTRUCTIONS:

- Read through the chapter review together.

Enter into God's presence.

Prayers that accomplish kingdom purposes come from people who know God intimately. Our relationship with the Lord is the most important thing about us. The Father's reward in this secret place of Alone Prayer cannot be found in any other pursuit.

Personal intimate prayer is the flame that ignites powerful Unified Prayer. Pray in secret when alone. Pray together when together. Pray alone, pray together. This prayer rhythm enriches the Bride of Christ as we are knit together for kingdom purposes.

Call on God's power.

We pray from faith and walk away from worry, knowing that our heavenly Father cares for our needs. Attention on heavenly pursuits is the thread that runs through our prayers as we seek His kingdom first.

Unified Prayer is an essential element of a faith-filled body of believers. A healthy church family is active in constant prayer.

The spiritual battles are intense. The time to pray is now! We are being summoned to join the tactical forces of Unified Prayer. This is how we gain victory over enemy tactics, marching in sync with each other. Initiate Unified Prayer whenever possible. Call friends over for a time of prayer. Volunteer to lead prayer in your small group. Grab friends before church to pray together. Be the one who turns the tide that awakens believers around you to pray.

Enter in.

Enter the Lord's presence with worship. Offering our sacrifice of praise before we introduce any petition is the appropriate way to approach our King. Praise is as simple as saying what we know is true about God as we reflect on who God is and the wondrous aspects of His nature. "Lord, you are God." "Lord, you made us, and we are yours." "Lord, you are the Good Shepherd." "You are King, and we offer you thanksgiving and praise."

Building Blocks for Unified Prayer:

1. **Together:** We are the body of Christ. *Praying out loud joins us together in faith.*

2. **Family:** We are brothers and sisters in Christ. *Conversation in prayer joins us together in love.*

3. **Unity:** We are one in Christ. *Agreement in prayer joins us together in unity.*

Open the door to the House of Prayer and look inside. We see believers gathered. This is where praying disciples think of Unified Prayer as essential to their community. Where is this House of Prayer? Church building, home, small group location, workplace, marketplace, everywhere. The House of Prayer is anywhere believers are together

Come on in. Jesus is here.

Let's Talk About It

INSTRUCTIONS:

- Read each Scripture.

- Use the accompanying question to discuss how the Scripture relates to prayer.

"Make your ways known to me, Lord; teach me your paths. Guide me in your truth and teach me, for you are the God of my salvation; I wait for you all day long." (Psalm 25:4 - 5)

Take one phrase from Psalm 25:4 - 5 and make it a prayer by saying the words of the phrase, and then expounding on the thought.

"Rejoice always, pray constantly, give thanks in everything; for this is God's will for you in Christ Jesus. Don't stifle the Spirit." (1 Thessalonians 5:16 - 21)

What is God's will for us regarding prayer? What should we expect to happen when joyful, prayerful, and thankful believers are in the same place at the same time?

"Jesus came near and said to them, 'All authority has been given to me in heaven and on earth. Go, therefore, and make disciples of all nations, baptizing them in the name of the Father and of the Son and of the Holy Spirit, teaching them to observe everything I have commanded you. And remember, I am with you always, to the end of the age.'" (Matthew 28:18 - 20)

What part does Unified Prayer have in obeying Jesus' commission to make disciples? Where is Jesus when our voices are one in a prayer conversation?

Let's Talk About It More (as time allows)

"I have asked one thing from the Lord; it is what I desire: to dwell in the house of the Lord all the days of my life, gazing on the beauty of the

Lord and seeking him in his temple. For he will conceal me in his shelter in the day of adversity; he will hide me under the cover of his tent; he will set me high on a rock. Then my head will be high above my enemies around me; I will offer sacrifices in his tent with shouts of joy. I will sing and make music to the Lord. Lord, hear my voice when I call; be gracious to me and answer me. My heart says this about you: 'Seek his face.' Lord, I will seek your face." (Psalm 27:4 - 8)

How does the Lord reward those who abide with Him in Alone Prayer?

____

"Therefore I tell you: Don't worry about your life, ... Consider the birds of the sky: They don't sow or reap or gather into barns, yet your heavenly Father feeds them. Aren't you worth more than they? Can any of you add one moment to his life span by worrying? ... So don't worry, saying, 'What will we eat?' or 'What will we drink?' or 'What will we wear?' For the Gentiles eagerly seek all these things, and your heavenly Father knows that you need them. But seek first the kingdom of God and his righteousness, and all these things will be provided for you. Therefore don't worry about tomorrow, because tomorrow will worry about itself." (Matthew 6:25 - 34)

How does seeking first the kingdom of God keep us from worry? Why are we able to pray from faith instead of praying from worry?

____

"Take the helmet of salvation and the sword of the Spirit—which is the word of God. Pray at all times in the Spirit with every prayer and request, and stay alert with all perseverance and intercession for all the saints." (Ephesians 6:17 - 18)

Who is being summoned to join the tactical forces of Unified Prayer? Is this assignment optional for us who believe? Why or why not?

____

"After they were released, they went to their own people and reported everything ... When they heard this, they raised their voices together to God and said, 'Master, you are the one who made the heaven, the earth, and the sea, and everything in them.'" (Acts 4:23 - 24)

These Christians have just experienced threats and persecution. How do they start their prayer? Why do you think they start their prayer this way?

Practical Challenge

THREE SEEDS TO PLANT

What are three concepts or practices regarding Alone Prayer and Unified Prayer that the Holy Spirit is impressing on you to incorporate into your life right now? Think of these ideas as *seeds* to plant and water, asking the Lord to bring growth.

Write these three seeds as action steps. For example, "Make a commitment to spend time in Alone Prayer every day." "Ask the Holy Spirit to give me a few words to say in Unified Prayer at our Sunday School class." "As leader of a small group, I will invest in Unified Prayer at the beginning of our gathering instead of hurried prayer at the end."

1. ______________________________

2. ______________________________

3. ______________________________

Bring these action steps to the Lord in your times of Alone Prayer, asking Him to lead you in obedience to His will, for spiritual growth that pleases Him. Meet with one or two Christ-follower friends to pray about these seeds together.

Name: ______________________________

Date: ______________________________

HOUSE OF PRAYER

End Notes

Chapter 1: *Call to Prayer*

1. S. D. Gordon, *Quiet Talks on Prayer* (London: Fleming H. Revell, 1904), 12.

Chapter 2: *Foundation*

2. S. D. Gordon, *Quiet Talks on Prayer* (London: Fleming H. Revell, 1904), 150.
3. S. D. Gordon, *Quiet Talks on Prayer* (London: Fleming H. Revell, 1904). 150.
4. Leonard Ravenhill, *Heart Breathings...in Poetry and Prose* (HCP, 1995)

Chapter 3: *Framework*

5. Samuel Isenhower, *The 3 Keys of Availing Prayer* (Upward Press, 2016*), 17.
6. S. D. Gordon, *Quiet Talks on Prayer* (London: Fleming H. Revell, 1904), 138.
7. S. D. Gordon, *Quiet Talks on Prayer* (London: Fleming H. Revell, 1904), 182.
8. Andrew Murray, *With Christ in the School of Prayer* (NY: Fleming H. Revell, 1885), 86.
9. Samuel Isenhower, *The 3 Keys of Availing Prayer* (Upward Press, 2016*), 1.

Chapter 4: *Together*

10. Andrew Murray, *With Christ in the School of Prayer* (NY: Fleming H. Revell, 1885), 85.

11. Andrew Murray, *With Christ in the School of Prayer* (NY: Fleming H. Revell, 1885), 84.

Chapter 5: *Family*

12. Andrew Murray, *With Christ in the School of Prayer* (NY: Fleming H. Revell, 1885), 83.
13. S. D. Gordon, *Quiet Talks on Prayer* (London: Fleming H. Revell, 1904), 161.
14. D. L. Moody, *Prevailing Prayer* (Chicago: Moody Publishers, 1941), 19.

Chapter 6: *Unity*

15. R. A. Torrey, *Torrey On Prayer* (Alachua, FL: Bridge-Logos Foundation, 2009), 119.

Chapter 7: *Established*

16. Leonard Ravenhill, *Revival Sermons: Meat for Men* (Fires of Revival, 1961).
17. Andrew Murray, *With Christ in the School of Prayer* (NY: Fleming H. Revell, 1885), 22.
18. Andrew Murray, *With Christ in the School of Prayer* (NY: Fleming H. Revell, 1885), 8.
19. R. A. Torrey, *Torrey On Prayer* (Alachua, FL: Bridge-Logos Foundation, 2009), 108.
20. E. M. Bounds, *Power through Prayer*, 1910 (Christian Classics Ethereal Library:ccel.org), 54.
21. S. D. Gordon, *Quiet Talks on Prayer* (London: Fleming H. Revell, 1904), 17.
22. Andrew Murray, *With Christ in the School of Prayer* (NY: Fleming H. Revell, 1885), 177.

* available on request from samisenhower@gmail.com

Acknowledgements

> Trust in the Lord with all your heart, and do not lean on your own understanding. In all your ways acknowledge him, and he will make straight your paths. (Proverbs 3:5 - 6 ESV)

The first one to acknowledge is the Lord Jesus, for taking me under His wing to teach me. I am grateful to Him for putting a message on my heart and for placing people in my life to assist in putting that message into a book.

The direction, encouragement, and patience of my husband Steve made all this possible for me. In his kind manner he would tell me, "I know what you mean, but I'm not sure others will understand." His honest critiques help me strive for clarity. Steve also photographed my sketches and spent more hours than I know on post processing to format the photos of the sketches for the book. I'm grateful!

Oscar Dominguez, my pastor, and his wife Charlie listened to me when I first considered writing on this subject. Their enthusiasm has kept me pushing forward. I keep remembering Pastor Oscar's smile and nod when I said, "Every small group is a greenhouse for prayer life development."

The contributions of our three children are significant. Our daughter Melody Fernandez went through my very first manuscript draft with me. She challenged me to make sure every concept I write about is grounded in Scripture. I thank her for not allowing me to take the easy road of just writing my own thoughts. Daniel also read the early drafts and gave much-needed advice on clarity of doctrine and sound biblical teaching. Samuel not only designed the cover of the book but has also been my go-to person for anything about publishing. Samuel's heart for prayer has significantly influenced my approach to prayer.

Everyone needs a praying friend like Wende Gaikema. She has prayed with me from the time this book was no more than a faint idea all the way to the finish line. I am deeply grateful for all the friends and family members who have prayed for the Lord to direct this process. I am confident the Lord has heard their prayers.

The small group from our church that meets in our home every week became a testing ground for the *Group Review and Unified Prayer Guide.* I am grateful for the participation of these dear brothers and sisters in Christ.

What a blessing David and Laurie Beauchamp have been, with David as my copy editor, and Laurie with her insightful feedback for all the extra writing parts that need to fit in and on the book. They have been the sounding board, encouragers, and good friends that I've needed.

A handful of people encouraged me to illustrate the book with my own ink and watercolor sketches. I especially thank Jerry and Jan Engler, Margy Brand and my other friends in the neighborhood watercolor group, my sisters Mary Suptic and Barbara Crockett, my son Daniel, and my husband Steve. Each of them helped put this in the realm of possibility.

For the sketches: I thank my neighbors Tommy and Keleen Hays for giving me permission to sketch their beautiful greenhouse. Geneva Green allowed me to borrow a microphone from church, Laurie Beauchamp knitted a sample swatch, and my grandson Ari let me borrow his wooden train. All so I could do another sketch.

Of course, there are more people who have invested in this project along the way, too many to name. I appreciate each one the Lord has included in this journey.

My heart is full of gratitude.

About the Author

KAREN M. ISENHOWER is married to Steve, her lifelong companion, prayer partner, and primary encourager. They enjoy life on their little piece of Texas Hill Country. Their three married children have given them ten treasured grandchildren, all being nurtured to love and serve the Lord.

Developing artistic skills is an ongoing pursuit for Karen. She is a classically trained 'cellist, and an accomplished handweaver on full-size Swedish weaving looms. She also keeps a practice of documenting her day with simple ink and watercolor sketches in a daily sketchbook.

Karen holds a BMA degree in music education, with a minor in 'cello performance. She writes instructional and inspirational content for handweavers on her website and has been published four times in Handwoven Magazine.

Karen loves to pray for people; but even more, she loves to pray *with* people. She enjoys teaching about prayer; but even more, she enjoys inspiring people to ask the Lord to teach them to pray.

Printed in Great Britain
by Amazon

48205078R00096